Master Data Management
In a Nutshell

(Revised Edition)

Amit Khera

First Edition: October 2022

Revised Edition: April 2023

For my Parents – my role models

For my brothers Aman and Anupam – my motivators

For Preeti, Aadi, and Anav – my support

About the Author

Amit has over 24 years of industry experience across geographies and industry domains in implementing Master Data Management solutions. He has advised many organizations in Information Management programs and has donned multiple roles including Advisor, Architect, and Delivery Management. He has experience in anchoring customer transformation journeys for data-driven organizations, focusing on building solutions for accelerated business outcomes.

LinkedIn: https://in.linkedin.com/in/amit-khera-108b328

Contents at a Glance

Table of Contents

Preface

Data is becoming the world's new natural resource. The ability to understand data, process it, extract value from it, visualize it, and communicate it, is what enterprises are working on for enhanced business outcomes. The view on organizations' data plays a significant role in mitigating risks and cutting down costs. With businesses undergoing digital transformation globally, the CFOs now have a solid handle on data and analytics and are the strategic advisor to the CEO on what impact customer satisfaction has on the business. The industry today has shifted its focus from technology to business and processes where prioritizing customer experience is the "motto" to drive revenue. The organization understands that reliable and well-managed data is essential to success in a competitive market.

Master Data Management combines governance, processes, and technologies to define an accurate, timely, and consistent 360-degree view of master data across multiple business processes, external business partners, and application systems. The Master Data Management platform is expected to have data governance, information quality, modeling, stewardship, multi-domain, reference data, integrability, security, data protection, workflow, and visualization capabilities Whether the organization is managing customers, products, arrangements, locations, or master information about any other entities, they are dealing with datasets containing errors and duplicates. Leveraging AI and machine learning algorithms to automate the integration process empowers organizations to get hold of volume and variety of different data sources but not the data which they can trust for decisions.

Master Data Management, in a Nutshell, provides a simplified approach that gives you a perspective on how to approach MDM programs and pertains to best practices and standards in business process architecture, design, and quality management. The new insights available from various sources into MDM are allowing organizations to improve their services and a logical starting point for data analysis and analytics for data lakes and cloud data stores initiatives.

Improvements

Any feedback, or suggestions for improvement please write to amitpk.khera@outlook.com

Chapter 1: Master Data and Management

Today's data is an asset and organizations rely on their data assets to make more effective decisions and to operate more efficiently. Data is now being recognized as an area consisting of distinct categories with unique characteristics. If these characteristics are not properly understood, practitioners can only use generic approaches that are unlikely to deliver the desired results and may even be doomed to failure from the start in data-driven initiatives.

Data is broadly separated into three categories: Master, Transactional, and Analytical. In any organization, these are going to be commonly recognized concepts that are the focus of business processes, related to customers, products, suppliers, vendors, employees, finances, policies, and more. **Master data** represents a company's business vocabulary, covering the business entities, terminology, definitions, and classifications used to describe business information. As an example of customer domain, master data includes customer identity, profile, demographics, relationships with other customers (both individual and corporate), credit history, account relationships, privacy preferences, channel preferences, etc. **Transactional data** includes balances, principal, premiums, interest accrued, claims, invoices, withdrawals, payments, deposits, transfers, sales status, service tickets, etc. **Analytical data** include derived information such as trends, forecasts, sales history, buying patterns, profitability, segmentation, lifetime value, risk exposure, and so on.

Master Data includes the core business objects which constitute the enterprise's data assets. The master objects are those key "things" that matter the most—the things that are logged in our transaction systems, measured, and reported on in our reporting systems, and analyzed in our analytical systems. It is sometimes challenging for an organization to decide which data items should be treated as master data. It is better to categorize the data in terms of their behavior and attributes within the context of the business needs to decide on what entity types should be treated as master data. Historically, business applications were designed to meet operational needs for specific areas of business focus. The application architecture evolved organically to support the operations of each line of business and has been aligned for vertical success. Lines of business maintain their business information, channel variance further scatters business information, and variance in business information further fragments master data. Mergers and acquisitions suffer from the worst of all inputs. As a result, the "enterprise" is often composed of many applications referring to multiple sets of data that are intended to represent the same, or similar, business concepts. Alternatively, the same or similar names are used to refer to completely distinct concepts. This is the first **driver for Master Data Management—** the ability to rationalize the definitions and meanings of commonly used business concepts when possible and the ability to differentiate different business terms when they do not refer to the same concept. It is the basis for the high-value, core information that is used to enable better business processes across enterprises.

A single source of master data represents three important capabilities-

a. An authoritative source of information, a well-defined structure where the data has been standardized, duplicates have been rationalized, and the information is maintained through continuous or periodic updates.
b. The ability to use the information consistently, the information is complete, secure, accurate, and trusted to be high-quality and
c. The ability to evolve the master data and the management of master data to accommodate changing business needs.

Master Data Management is about the common meaning and sharing stable data to improve business efficacy. A few of the benefits of Master data management include-

a. Improved customer service

b. Consistent reporting
c. Regulatory Compliance
d. Privacy and Data Protection
e. Safety and Security (AML, KYC)
f. Improved risk management
g. Improved operational efficiency
h. Reduced costs
i. Improved decision-making
j. Increased information quality and
k. Regulatory compliance

1.1 Industry Views of MDM

Financial Services, Banking, and Insurance

The financial services industry has been one of the early adopters of MDM concepts and technologies to re-platform from legacy system environments to a functionally rich environment and effectively use customer analytics, customer behavior, and the factors enforcing customer brand loyalty, the propensity to buy, and reasons for customer attrition.

With financial services organizations given the mandate of several regulations such as the FATCA, KYC, AML, etc., the need to have accurate, complete, secure, and available master data about customers, their portfolios, transactions, sales, and service records became a mandatory requirement. The mergers and acquisitions (M&A) of financial services institutions have grown multifold and as such have consolidated multiple lines of businesses within their organizations. As an example, a multi-line retail bank grew by many acquisitions over the last multiple years. It ended up with 100 million accounts to manage which includes savings and deposit business, credit card business, and brokerage business. Another example of a commercial bank ended up with millions of customers across different LOBs, which includes corporate finance, cash trade, real estate loans, equipment leasing, and so on.

The use cases for banking customers include-

a. How can banks improve customer service and maintain customer relationships?
b. How can banks provide supporting products and services to meet Customer needs?
c. How do banks maintain excellent service levels in compliance to regulatory requirements with minimum cost and generate maximum revenues?
d. In the case of a new acquisition, how can banks ensure that systems are flexible enough to allow them to change business models quickly and easily?

A multi-line insurance company wants to transform into an integrated services company, offering not only traditional life insurance and property & casualty insurance products, but also a complete view of insurance providers, insurance agencies, insurance brokers, and third-party administrators. The insurance company needs to understand

a. How can we support the insurance coverage needs of our customers?
b. How can we best sell products and services to meet those needs while maintaining proper risk levels?
c. Household relationships and so on.

Retail

Retail stores use MDM to know their customers better and faster credit decisions, minimize fraud and gather business intelligence about the customer's spending patterns. Market basket analytics is an example where the relationships between correlated products that are often purchased together are maintained by MDM (the website offers products that are often purchased with the product the customer search was originally focused on). Retail stores often tackle multiple domains which include customer, location, product, and supplier. The typical use cases include

a. Improve customer service and satisfaction to build branding and add value for our customers
b. Maximize revenues and minimize costs
c. Keep track of consumer product needs
d. Maintain invoice and billing data
e. Householding and relationships aspects of the customer's profile
f. Streamline processes around all aspects of retail management in a retail organization such as buyers, merchandisers, sales, stores, and suppliers.
g. Automate workflows, standardize process governance, and quick turnarounds in the new product introduction process

Manufacturing

Manufacturing companies commonly focus on MDM Product domain solutions to support complex supply-chain requirements. Bill of Materials (BOM) is an essential element of master data for many manufacturing organizations. Manufacturing companies also endeavor to enable distribution channels for their products and services to serve individual consumers or businesses. Complete, accurate, and holistic information about their products and customers is necessary for a Manufacturing unit to eliminate the impacts on the efficiency of marketing, risk management, and ultimately profitability. A Manufacturing company had many business lines that run autonomously and control its profit-and-loss outcomes and need to track information for

a. Customers, suppliers, distributors
b. Parts required in the process and maintained the specifications of parts
c. and products
d. Shipping and invoicing information for customers and vendors

Telecommunication

Telecommunications companies deal with customers that include individuals as well as business entities. For Individual customer support, the use cases are like Retail. Telecom companies needed to look at ways to understand their customers better, including their total household relationships and the associated accounts as a combined household for effective sales campaigns to up-sell or cross-sell the right products. Telecommunication companies are investing in

a. To create innovative products and services
b. Improve customer service and satisfaction
c. Maximize revenue and minimize cost and more…
d. Holistic view of the telecommunication company's products, assets, and locations
e. Specific offers to the customer groups and locations that meet asset and resource qualifications criteria (Ex. Network Requirements)
f. Personalized, specially configured, and priced service packages

Healthcare and Pharmaceutical Industry

Patient & Provider MDM solutions are the typical MDM solutions within healthcare. The healthcare ecosystem includes hospitals, providers, insurance companies (payers), and pharmacies (this is where healthcare overlaps with the pharmaceutical industry). Pharmaceutical companies see MDM as an enabler to reconcile various industry-standard identifiers, thus creating an integrated view of the customer (physician, healthcare provider organization, and medical group). Pharmaceutical companies do not deal directly with consumers. They deal with physicians and service providers, who prescribe the company's products to their customers (patients). Pharmacy health information exchanges enable physicians and pharmacists to electronically exchange prescription information.

Public Services

To ensure the economic health, welfare, and security of their citizens, MDM-enabled solutions around master entities such as Citizens or Clients, Social Services, and Agencies can be used by the government to relate all information related to Tax and Revenue Information, Persons, Business, Identity, and Relationship Information, Healthcare and Social Services Information, Law Enforcement Information and Interaction and Transaction History. This will enable better customer service as processes take less citizen time and are better tailored to their needs.

Travel Services

Travel organizations include airlines, hotels, cars, cruise lines, customer, and vendor management. Travel organizations are investing in doing analysis and analytics to improve relationships with travelers (customers), provide the best offer, and provide best-in-class service with improvement in margins. The Master data solution covers travelers, their demographic details, carriers, agencies, contacts, travel preferences, and target marketing. Party, Product, Account, and location master generally need to be mastered

Others

Industry segments such as Energy, Gas, and utility companies also have similar drivers and challenges to support their customer base.

1.2 MDM and Data Warehousing

There is a very common debate within Customer organizations on why they need MDM solutions when there is an Enterprise data warehouse in their landscape or a project in flight with multiple data marts based on business needs. There are also discussions on the repeat effort required to spend MDM solution when data transformation and cleansing are already done through the ETL process for data warehousing. The ask is significant, and the simple answer is "The MDM solution and data warehouse have different use cases and complement each other. The business value increased multifold while having MDM and EDW in landscape". A more sophisticated, enterprise-wide view of the organization is provided through the combination of MDM and Data warehouses. The data warehouse provides a multidimensional collection of enterprise current and historical information which enables business intelligence for strategic decisions, determining trends, and creating forecasts. The MDM systems ensure consistent master information across transactional and analytical systems by maintaining the data warehouse dimensional tables. MDM can be real-time or near real-time while a data warehouse can have a time delay while data is collected. The organizational focus on MDM and governance directly benefits data warehouse usability and acceptance.

1.3 Data Warehouse and Data Lakes

A data warehouse is a database that is used and optimized for analytical purposes. The data from all relevant sources are brought together in the same structure and stored in a centralized location using the ETL process. ETL process stands for Extract, Transform, and Load. The goal of our data warehouse is-

a. Centralized location where the data from different data sources is available in a consistent manner.
b. Data visualizations on top of our data warehouse to understand the data and make better decisions for the organization

In the modern warehouse, we have Google Big Query, Snowflake, and Amazon Redshift which we see customers are leveraging for analytics leveraging MDM solutions. Big Query is a fully managed serverless data warehouse provided by Google. Snowflake is an analytic data warehouse provided by Snowflake as software, and as a service. Redshift is a service provided by Amazon.

We observed occasionally businesses have misconceptions about a data lake and data warehouse. The business view is that a data warehouse is a centralized location for data, the same thing is true for a data lake. Data warehouses and Data lakes are two different technologies. They are not mutually exclusive, and one technology is not replacing another. Data lakes are for raw data and unstructured data which cover JSON, images, and even videos. The volume of data is large with different data structures and data technologies, and different big data technologies are to be used for data exploration.

Organizations are extracting and placing data into data lakes without first transforming the data the way they would for an EDW. The organizations are deferring the transformation process, cleaning up data, and developing schema until they identify a clear business need. (ELT Pattern). The data lake has immense potential but there is a very real danger that the data lake turns into a garbage dump if there are no thoughts as to how the data will be used. With four basic ingredients, the data lake can be turned into an information gold mine -

Metadata. The analyst uses metadata to decipher the raw data found in the data lake. Metadata is the basic roadmap of data that resides in the data lake

Integration Mapping. The integration map is a detailed specification that shows how the data in the data lake can be integrated. The integration map shows how the isolation of the data in silos can be overcome.

Context. If you are going to put text in the data lake, then you must insert context as well, or at least a way to find that context.

Metaprocess. Metaprocess tags are information about the processing of data in the data lake.

****

Chapter 2: How to start your MDM Initiative

MDM initiatives are different from technology focus attempts at enterprise data consolidation like CRM or LOB-specific CIF. The focus is not necessary to create another silo but rather have a business focus to integrate methods for managed access to a consistent, unified view of enterprise data objects. Master Data Management is a business-led technology-enabled discipline to ensure organizations share consistent and accurate data. The value and need of MDM are known but still, companies often struggle to fully implement MDM. Most companies are making mistakes with the approach to considering MDM as a Data Integration discipline only.

A business case for MDM remains a significant challenge for most organizations. For an MDM initiative driven by business, the imperative for a change comes from executive management. Financial services, telecommunication, or retail company might initially centralize the data around customers to help facilitate up-sell and cross-sell to the customer base. Manufacturers or distributors might first centralize data around the product to optimize the supply chain cost and delivery. A healthcare company may want to focus on a Master Patient Index solution to manage information about patients and healthcare providers.

2.1 Business Problems and Objectives

Business Problems	Business Objectives
Lack of Enterprise view of data resulting in less effective cross-sell and upsell	Create a golden record of the customer as a foundation for effective servicing and cross-selling
Customer information is different on the delivery channel	Improve data quality and data inconsistencies to provide a consistent experience for consumers across delivery channels

The same data update needs to be made in multiple systems	Gain operational efficiencies by reducing duplicate data
Different terminology, values, and format of the same data result in misinterpretation of the information	MDM solution, standard taxonomy, simplify ongoing integration and new development

Figure 1 Business Alignments

The key step for MDM initiatives is to have alignment with businesses and stakeholders to define what is to be achieved and why are the project sponsors undertaking this effort. Calculating the ROI of a Master Data Management (MDM) program is a crucial step in the journey. It is of utmost importance to deliver tangible values to the business and depict the practical utility that a system offers. MDM program's momentum can slow down if enabling factors, needed capabilities, and improvements are not achieved. Successful programs begin with a series of tightly scoped initiatives with clearly articulated business value and sponsorship. It is beneficial to engage key business stakeholders and sponsors from the start to identify critical business problems and/or business imperatives and to realize the business objectives of the MDM solution.

2.2 Master Data, Reference Data, and Metadata

It is important to understand the difference between Master data, Reference data, and Metadata before starting an MDM initiative. **Master data** is the consistent and uniform set of objects, identifiers, attributes, and rules that describe the core (and relatively stable) entities of the enterprise and that is used across multiple business processes. **Reference data** is focused on defining and distributing collections of common values to be used in lookups to ensure the consistent use of a code such as product code, state code, customer life cycle status or account type codes, transaction codes, and so on. **Metadata** is information about the data collected, what data or information exists, where it is being used, what is the business definition, why we need that, when it was last updated, and how it is interrelated to other information.

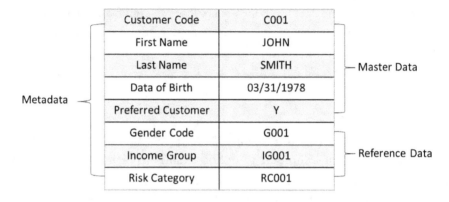

Figure 2 Metadata and Master Data

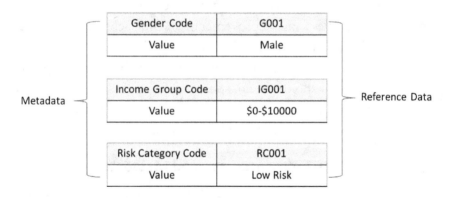

Figure 3 Metadata and Reference Data

Master data and reference data are often thought of as the same. The reality is that they are quite different, even though they have strong dependencies on each other. Failure to recognize these differences is risky, particularly given the current explosion of interest in master data.

There are three kinds of reference data, namely-

a. Things external to the enterprise, such as country codes, tax rates, ISO, ANSI, etc.
b. Things internal to the enterprise, such as type codes, status codes, role codes, and customer type
c. Classification schemes, such as market segment classifications and industry classifications.

Reference data management guarantees the common value of an object and is used in a read-only manner by operational, analytical, and definitional systems. Cross-enterprise reference data needs to be reconciled for master data management initiatives.

2.3 MDM Dimensions

Master Domains vary from industry to industry. The Banking and Insurance industry may wish to consider their customer, accounts, product, and policies as master data. The Retail industry might be interested in considering distribution channels, customers, suppliers, referrers, employees, or internal organizations. The Manufacturing may be focused on managing suppliers, customers, distributors, products, Materials, Items, or locations. Telecommunication companies may be concerned with customers, accounts, tower locations, and services. For Healthcare, this master data would be Members, Providers, Products, Claims, or Clinical and for Travel master, data can be passengers, carriers, parts, regulatory agencies, and contacts within these organizations. It is important to identify who will be the primary consumer of the master data to define patterns of use.

There are three primary dimensions of the Master Data Management solution. This includes

a. what master data need to manage (master data domains) – This covers customer, product, account, location, and other Master domains
b. how to use the master data (pattern of use) – This covers

collaborative, operational, and analytical MDM, and

c. how to architect the solution (implementation style) – This covers consolidation, registry, coexistence, and transactional MDM implementation styles

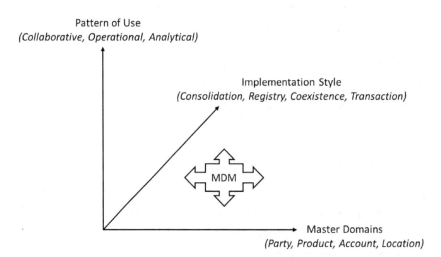

Figure 4 MDM Dimensions

Companies have grown to depend on multiple systems: ERP, warehouse, e-commerce, call center, CRM, accounting—the list goes on. With the importance of trustworthy and timely data on the rise and the mandate to align with enterprise information management (EIS) strategy, multi-Domain MDM enables an integrated and modern approach to mastering data based on a single, seamless technology platform. Multidomain MDM is concerned with managing master data across multiple domains. Customer, Product, Locations, Finance, and Employee domains have been among the most targeted data domains where MDM initiatives are focused.

The focus on these domains has evolved from data management practices associated with customer data integration (CDI), product integration management (PIM), accounts receivable (AR), and human resources (HR). Venturing into multi-domain MDM becomes a large exercise in Business Process Management (BPM) and Change

Management. The planning and adoption of cross-functional disciplines and processes necessary for the support of MDM need to be well orchestrated.

Here are a few industry-oriented examples of how domains are often defined

a. Financial Services: Customers, Accounts, Products, Locations
b. Manufacturing: Customers, Products, Suppliers, Materials, Items, Locations
c. Healthcare: Members, Providers, Products, Claims, Clinical, Actuarial

Industries today are referencing libraries of common standards to define the domain such as FpML for financial products, HL7 for the pharmaceutical industry, ACORD for the insurance industry, GS1 for the retail industry, or EDIX for cross-industry that describe entities for business-to-business (B2B).

The below factors determine what domains need to be Master by an organization

a. Business Value, each domain needs to be evaluated from business value to determine the benefits of applying MDM to it
b. Volume, each domain to be evaluated with the need for MDM automation. Ex, if a company offers one hundred products, is there any business value in mastering the product
c. Volatility, if the data in a particular domain does not change, it is unlikely to need MDM
d. Reusability, more a domain used across an enterprise, the higher the probability of benefits from MDM
e. Complexity, the complexity of data associated with the domain is directly proportional to MDM benefits.

Master data entities play a significant role in the enterprise data model. They connect all major entities and help an organization relate its information. The scope of the Master Data Management solution by its very nature is extremely broad and applies equally well to customer-centric, product-centric, and reference data–centric business problems from strategic and tactical perspectives. The architecture should be data-driven as it's not just application design, but operational maintenance and business decisions revolve around data. Getting insights into data can make a tremendous difference to an organization's profitability. Dashboard to visualize the metrics from server log data, sending alerts in the case of issues and triggering the auto-healing mechanism, collecting overall data, and feeding to the machine learning algorithm to forecast future possible issues helps to increase customer satisfaction and maximize the return on your investment. Remember MDM is for the business, by the IT.

2.4 MDM Implementation Style

When implementing an MDM system one of the key decisions to be made is the choice of MDM Implementation Style. Gartner describes four styles of MDM Hub: Registry Hub, Consolidation Hub, Coexistence Hub, and Transaction Hub. MDM projects need to carefully evaluate the benefits and risks associated with each approach and decide on the appropriate balance of these factors for implementing an MDM solution in a phased, risk-managed fashion. A business must decide which implementation style delivers the appropriate business value while still considering implementation cost. The Data Hub of Registry style stores only key identifiers and links them to the fragments of master data in source systems. The Consolidation style mainly involves the aggregation of master data and is generally used to support analysis. The Coexistence Hub architecture style of the Data Hub physically stores some master data along with referencing some other data in the source systems. The Transaction Hub physically stores the master entities and is used as the authoritative system of record for master data.

Registry Style

The Registry Implementation Style provides a read-only source of master data to consuming applications. An MDM System deployed with this implementation style enables a set of attributes (Critical Data Elements) needed to uniquely identify a master data entity leveraging match and merge capabilities.

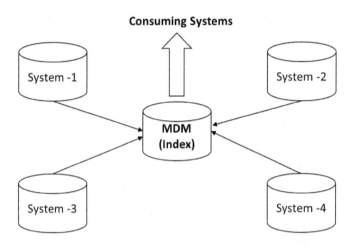

Figure 5 Registry Style

Data is not sent back to source systems and is linked from the MDM System using cross-reference keys. Registry style is the lowest-cost master data integration solution. The master data is managed in the source system and governance is required to ensure a reliable golden record in the MDM system.

Critical Data Elements (CDEs) are defined as "the data that is critical to an organization's success" within the context of each business application use. Critical data elements help companies to quickly deliver business value by focusing on the most critical data. CDEs are used for establishing information and business policy compliance, and they must be subjected to governance in an MDM environment

Consolidation Style

With a Consolidation style, data is consolidated into the MDM hub from multiple sources to create a high-quality single version of the truth of data. This data can then be cleansed, matched, and integrated to offer a complete single record for one or more master data domains.

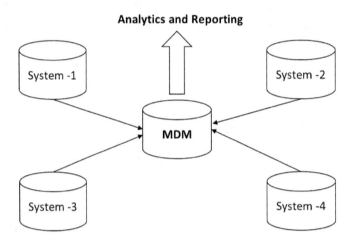

Figure 6 Consolidation Style

The consolidation style leverages the MDM hub as a reference point for analytics and reporting. Consolidated hubs are inexpensive and quick to set up, providing a fast and efficient way to facilitate enterprise-wide reporting. This style is mainly used for analysis, giving you a trusted golden record while the source systems can still maintain business as usual.

Coexistence Style

A Co-existence style allows you to construct a single version of the truth in the same way as the consolidation style does. The difference is that the hub stores master data while updates take place in the source systems. The synchronization between multiple source systems changing master data and the MDM System can be unidirectional (from system1 to MDM) or bidirectional (from system2 to MDM System and MDM to system1). Any change executed in the MDM System can be published to read-only, consuming applications of master data.

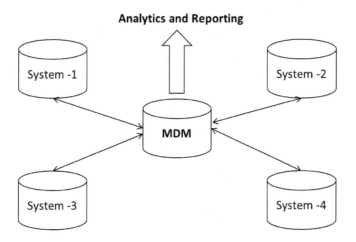

Figure 7 Coexistence Style

The Coexistence style can be more expensive to deploy than the Consolidation style as master data changes can happen in the MDM system as well as in the application systems. All attributes of the master data model must be consistent and cleansed before uploading them into the Master Data Management system, enabling a Single version of truth between MDM and source systems.

Transactional Style

The Transactional Hub MDM implementation style provides centralized and complete master data in a system of record where the hub becomes the single provider of master data. The master data attributes are stored and maintained in the MDM hub using linking, cleansing, matching, and enriching algorithms. The source systems can no longer create or update the master attributes. Master Data is authored in MDM and not in source systems. MDM is the sole provider of the source of truth. The Master Data attributes can be published back to their respective source system to give complete consistency. All systems must subscribe to the MDM hub for Master Data. This is a comprehensive solution that can be used to phase out obsolete legacy systems

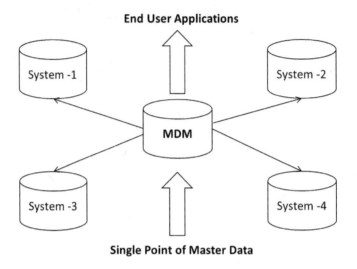

Figure 8 Transaction Style

2.5 Pattern of Use – How Master Data is Used

Companies typically use three main reasons to justify an MDM implementation which are Revenue growth, Risk management, and Cost reduction. The three reasons are directly aligned with the three primary MDM use patterns which includes Analytical MDM (for Revenue Growth), Operational MDM (Risk Management), and Enterprise MDM (Cost Reduction). These patterns are different patterns describing how the managed master data entities can be consumed. In the Analytical pattern, the MDM system is the source for analytical systems for reporting purposes. Under the Operational pattern, the MDM system participates in end-to-end business transactions which include operational transactions and business processes of the industry. With the Enterprise pattern, different business functions collaborate to manage the lifecycle of the master data. Role-based access control determines which roles can manage which aspect of the master data attributes.

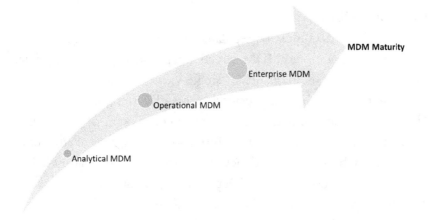

Figure 9 MDM use pattern

It is important to notice that the above figure does not suggest a sequence to be adopted when implementing an MDM solution. The phased deployments need to be observed. Not all MDM implementations are the same. Analytical, operational, and enterprise MDM offers different challenges from both IT infrastructure and business model perspectives. In practice, MDM usage will often cross the boundaries between different patterns of use. MDM program may start with the usage style that is important to achieving the business needs and additional styles can be incorporated to meet further requirements

Analytical MDM

Revenue growth is mostly related to better strategic decisions. The core objective of Analytical MDM is to support business processes and applications that use master data primarily to analyze business performance and provide appropriate reporting and analytical capabilities. Analytical MDM tends to be read mostly. The two most common Master Data Management hub styles for Analytical MDM are Registry Style and Consolidation Style. The downstream systems will have access to a cleansed, enriched, and integrated view of the data to perform deep analytics and provide drill-through capabilities

Operational MDM

The operational data must be regulated to minimize risk and increase compliance. Operational MDM targets operational systems and data. The core objective is to ensure a "single view" of master data in the core systems used by the business users. By design, Operational MDM systems ensure that the accurate, single version of the truth is maintained in the MDM Data Hub and propagated to the core systems used by existing and new processes and applications. The two most common Master Data Management hub styles for Operational MDM are Co-Existence and Transactional Style

Enterprise MDM

Enterprise MDM represents a combination of analytical and operational MDMs and must satisfy the diverse requirements of both. It integrates master data across multiple IT systems and businesses. The Enterprise MDM implementation is the recommended objective to achieve well-designed consistent entity definitions across the enterprises

2.6 Guiding Principles for MDM Initiative

The MDM program approach is different from other programs like Data Warehouse / BI Reporting or Core Processing systems. The data warehouse program's focus is on Information delivery requirements and usability. The core processing system emphasis is on Business processes and business rules. The essential to the successful MDM deployment are various technologies where the activity focus is on comprehensive information requirements and data quality.

The efforts are required to integrate multiple key components as mentioned below-

Figure 10 MDM Guiding Principles

Business Data Models

The business object model shows a unique perspective on the domain to be mastered. It describes a static representation of the business domain which includes the extent of the information the stakeholders envision being stored in the MDM solution. The term business object modeling should not be confused with enterprise modeling which covers the entire enterprise from different perspectives. The business object model is limited to the domain within the line of business and aligned to the use cases. The key benefit is to leverage business object models as it is built to make them understandable for the business and use terms, they are familiar with wherever possible. It also includes a glossary that helps identify double meanings and ensures agreement amongst stakeholders. We need to remember that the business will only be able to identify what data entities and elements they rely on as they always have a shallow and narrow view of data. Data must be profiled from technical and business points of view to understand which of the elements are critical to business and analytical operations. As part of the master data list, the business areas need to identify critical data elements

(CDEs) as this is a valuable subclassification for data quality assessment and business terms standardizations

Context Diagram

The context diagram should be leveraged to define who and what will be interacting with the MDM solution. The business and system context diagrams clarify the interfaces and boundaries of the project or process and unfold some very nasty surprises. The business context diagram identifies business areas that benefit from the MDM system. The system context diagram identifies the system that will source the information to MDM, interact with the MDM solution, and receive information from the MDM solution

Business Data Services

The success of MDM systems is to have the data reflected in the various applications and business processes. The downstream and upstream application systems are evaluated to identify what Business processes they are performing on MDM data. This also includes analyzing the value chain for the domain to identify applicable Business processes. While the MDM maintains the data, it is the business services that make the data universally available. It is unreasonable to think that the applications and operating systems will be changed to use an MDM data model. The business services should be based on data federation technologies. These technologies apply business and data rules before it is passed to the user of other applications. It is unique because not all businesses encounter the same kinds of market pressure, industry competition, and/or government regulations. The major drivers include

a. Provide a consistent enterprise view of data
b. Use a common and shared business vocabulary
c. Data is available to consumers easier and faster
d. Prevent investments in redundant systems
e. Facilitate consistent reporting

Data Integration

Data integration technologies surface the data in the format required by business users or applications. The goal is to offer uniform access to a set of data sources by integrating and transforming data on demand across multiple sources according to business requirements. Data Integration efficiently delivers data to all analytics systems and application-to-application data integration. It also centralizes data management, monitoring, and control to ensure that data moving through the hub is trustworthy, secure, and traceable to enable lineage for data quality issues. The most fundamental is to implement meta-data-driven data integration that captures the data syntax, semantics, and business rules relevant to integrating data.

Data Stewardship

The MDM system must be flexible to accommodate the business changes over time. Data stewards need to be closely aligned with the touch points and consumers of the master data and influence the need to change MDM system business processes or data delivery processes. There is an implicit relationship between data quality management, data governance, and data stewardship. For a successful MDM program, practices for all three need to be closely orchestrated. A data quality management framework is to apply concepts and practices to improve data and information quality which covers setting data quality policies and guidelines, data quality measurement, data quality analysis, data cleansing, and correction, data quality process improvement, and data quality education. Data governance encompasses the people, processes, and technology that are required to create a consistent enterprise view of data in an organization and creates a discipline to create and maintain high-quality data and a structure to plan, monitor, and enforce the management of data assets.

Entity Resolution

Entity resolution addresses the issues of multiple versions with similar data representing the same entity and encompasses process and technology to derive what common set of data elements should be used across multiple sources. Unique entity identification is a common theme across MDM initiatives. The degree of completeness, accuracy, and consistency of data decides the entity resolution outcome.

As an example, matching records about individuals is a relatively well-known problem, and several matching techniques and solutions use a variety of attributes of the individual (for example, name, address, date of birth, identifier, and other demographics attributes, if they are known) to deliver a high confidence matching result. Within the product domain, the challenge of identifying, matching, and linking entities is complex. This complexity is driven by the fact that, although product attributes may represent a standard set for each product category, different manufacturers or suppliers may use different expressions, abbreviations, and attribute values to describe the same feature. Similarly, in financial services, a similar product may be described differently. The techniques and approaches to entity resolution in the product domain are often based on semantic-driven rather than syntax-driven analysis.

2.7 MDM Implementation Considerations

Implementing MDM is never a big-bang approach. Master Data Management implementations are usually done in phases that follow the pattern to populate the MDM System with the initial data set followed by integrating additional downstream and upstream application systems that require access to master data at the Hub. The scope of the first phase must assure that the business stakeholder remains committed to the MDM journey and that a good return on investment can be shown in a relatively short amount of time. Subsequent phases then broaden the initial deployment by adding functionality or master data domains.

MDM project requires a certain degree of existing business process adaptation or reengineering for which the architecture patterns from the Enterprise Information Integration (EII) domain and the Enterprise Application Integration (EAI) domain would also be leveraged for an end-to-end solution. The enterprise must establish a strong Information Governance group working horizontally across all lines of business to reach a collective agreement on integration patterns, master data models, and how master data is used in business processes. Adequate information maturity and Information Governance are the foundation for a phased end-to-end rollout of MDM across an organization.

The other crucial factor for the success of MDM initiatives is executive-level support with an agreed return on investments. The MDM programs tend to become large very quickly as business learns the master domain importance within the journey. It is mandated to manage the scope. Think backward from the customers' needs, and determine what is critical for them, while also taking care of architectural constraints. It is advisable to divide customer requirements into "must-have" (Requirements without which the product cannot launch), "should have" (Requirements that are the most desirable), and "could have" (Requirements that are nice to have) categories and plan a minimum viable product (MVP) for your customer with must-have requirements and go for the next iteration of delivery with should-have requirements.

Taking an agile approach helps build a customer-centric product. There is also close coordination required between business and technology. We observed the challenge of procuring the right infrastructure and tools because of communication gaps which result in financial and timing impacts. Businesses must be on-boarded with defined ownership. Building technical capability now and selling to businesses later may not work, resulting in a lack of user adoption. MDM programs must be socialized to enterprises from day 1 with change management processes. Understanding source system processes, transformations and underestimating the impact is the biggest mistake. " The devil is in the details." The systems may seem simple, but the details are complicated and likely to delay the program.

Successful Master data Management is about having

a. Ownership defined, named persons are held accountable for the structure of Master Data and quality of data
b. Common definitions, the model having consistent definitions
c. Common unique identifying keys, having the same unique identifier for a Master Data item across processes
d. Defined system of record, source of trusted data
e. The data governance model defines governance roles, maintenance processes, data principles, data quality monitoring, and procedures for continuous improvement.
f. Choose the right product

****

Chapter 3: Choose your MDM product

In a rapid and competitive market, the selection of the right MDM tool plays a significant role in efficient solutions. A common thread among the solutions is the ability to create and maintain an accurate, timely, and authoritative "system of record" for a given subject domain. Each country and region have its laws and compliance regime, which MDM solution needs to adhere to. The selection of the right MDM tool is a critical step in ensuring the successful execution of the data strategy and achieving the desired objectives, bringing tremendous value to the organization.

There are multiple MDM COTS products in the market today in various categories as **leaders, visionaries, niche players, and challengers as defined by Gartner.** The MDM requirements should be agnostic of any vendor products and must define the solutions' capabilities. It is important to first define the organization's vision and objectives as to what organization wants to achieve with the MDM program and how is it complementing the overall enterprise-wide strategic solution data strategy. Documenting the key capabilities to enable, the high-level requirements, and use cases followed by the tool assessment help in making the correct decision for the selection of MDM tools. The usage and focus of master data for building, running, and reporting the business are playing a key role in the product selection process.

3.1 Product Evaluation Criteria

With organizations across industry verticals making significant investments in MDM solutions, it is necessary to recognize the capabilities different tools are providing to meet your organization's business needs. Please note that there is no specific order of evaluation, and all parameters have equal importance subject to alignment with the organization's priorities.

Below are the capabilities that you can use to compare requirements

Data Model

a. Multi-domain model support
b. Flexibility in data model configuration
c. Support relationships, hierarchies
d. Alignment with the industry data models
e. Reference data support

Core Capabilities

a. Built-in data governance capabilities
b. Process flow and workflow engine
c. Match and merge capabilities; global id generation
d. Version control
e. Audit controls
f. Business services
g. Change management
h. Rules of visibility – who can see what.

Database

a. Relational database
b. No SQL database
c. Graph database

Data Integration

a. Supports real or near real-time integration
b. Ability to load large volumes of data in a fast, efficient, and
c. Accurate manner
d. Import data from multiple sources as well as exporting features
e. Ease of integration with third-party products (integration capabilities with external/internal sources via APIs – cloud/on-premises solution)

Data Stewardship Support and Workflow

a. Self-service business interface capabilities for data steward–crud operations, match and merge, workflows, dashboards
b. Flexible and comprehensive workflow with multiple approvals

process

c. Data profiling capabilities

Business Resilience/ Disaster Recovery

a. Hardware/software resilience
b. Disaster recovery configurations

Technology and Architecture Considerations

a. Cloud adaptability
b. Vendor integrity
c. Multiple deployments (on-premises, cloud, hybrid)
d. Multiple implementation architectures/use cases
e. Backup policy

Performance, Scalability, and Availability

a. Ability to scale up based on customer's requirements (new master/reference data domains)
b. Availability of the MDM solution performance aspects
c. Support for rapid & agile model development
d. SOA architecture
e. Deployable on commodity hardware

Vendor Viability

a. Market responsiveness and Track record
b. Vendor's maturity
c. Vendor's financial health
d. Existing customers
e. Partners Ecosystem
f. Technical Support

Financial Considerations

a. Installation/licensing support
b. User license
c. Cost involved in the provision of the training of the installed product to the users
d. Product cost

3.2 Product Evaluation Approach

The key objective of the evaluation exercise is to identify the appropriate product that aligns with the organization's identified use cases. Below is the suggested approach for doing an MDM product evaluation

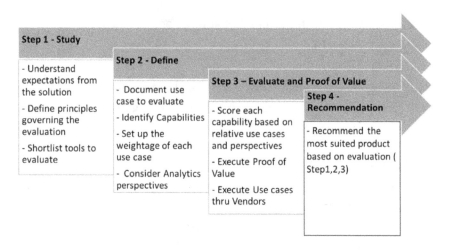

Step 1 - Study
- Understand expectations from the solution
- Define principles governing the evaluation
- Shortlist tools to evaluate

Step 2 - Define
- Document use case to evaluate
- Identify Capabilities
- Set up the weightage of each use case
- Consider Analytics perspectives

Step 3 – Evaluate and Proof of Value
- Score each capability based on relative use cases and perspectives
- Execute Proof of Value
- Execute Use cases thru Vendors

Step 4 - Recommendation
- Recommend the most suited product based on evaluation (Step1,2,3)

Figure 11 Product Evaluation Framework

Choosing the right vendor and solution can be a complicated process that requires in-depth research and often comes down to more than just the solution and its technical capabilities. When choosing an MDM product, look for products that are built on technologies that will carry your company through the next 10 years and not based on past technologies. Cloud-native architecture, Microservices, Graph databases, and AI are becoming mainstream, more mature, remarkably effective, and readily available technologies for MDM. Another aspect to consider is Change management. Once the data is pulled into the MDM repository, there will certainly be updates to the data. How the data will be maintained, and how the attributes will be added must be considered. Manual intervention in this process should be avoided.

A recent innovation in the MDM space is managing master data using a hosted or cloud-based environment instead of a traditional on-premises implementation. Cloud hosting is becoming the default for many computing solutions. There are cost efficiencies, agility benefits, and many other advantages that should be driving you to look at the cloud as a base for your current and future MDM implementations. Designing scalable, resilient, and performance architecture along with the automation approach, service-oriented architecture (SOA), and a data-driven approach are the major factors for businesses to adopt an MDM solution. It is always recommended to do proof of concept and prototype according to the business requirement assessment, and the agility, speed, and security of the application.

****

Chapter 4: MDM on Cloud

With all the interest surrounding Cloud, it is helpful to understand what is driving this need to change. Digital transformation is impacting every industry and business. Each IT organization has its unique drivers, but they generally fall into broad categories like cost, availability, time-to-market, etc. For non-IT organizations, there are pressures from the highest-level executives for more flexibility, doing more with less cost, and using the information as a competitive advantage. IT organizations are working towards transformation with greater business agility and adopting cloud over on-premises solutions to serve customers worldwide. These covers replace old technology, new application adoption, and move from CAPEX to OPEX.

4.1 Cloud Computing

Cloud computing architecture has become increasingly important these days where you have an end-to-end view of the frontend platforms, the application development platform, servers, storage, database, automation, delivery, and the networks that are required to manage the entire solution landscape. Cloud computing is divided into three types:

- **Infrastructure as a Service (IaaS)** is the most basic form where basic computing resources are provided, and the consumer installs and manages the needed software. This model gives the most control
- **Platform as a Service (PaaS) model** manages the underlying infrastructure. This service model refers to platforms that can be used to program applications by the consumer.
- **The vendor completely manages the software as a Service (SaaS) model.** The user can configure and use it through a web browser. Common examples are Google's services like Docs, Calendar, and Sheets or Microsoft Office 365.

There are new models called **Function as a Service (FaaS)** that fall somewhere in between. For example, the capability of being able to write a piece of code that executes based on triggers, like a web service call is somewhere between PaaS and SaaS. Another example is **containers**, which are a level above the operating system and somewhere between IaaS and PaaS. Some types of software come in all variants, like databases. You can install a database on an IaaS machine, use the same database as a PaaS offering, and, in some cases, even as a SaaS product.

Enterprises are collecting data from more and increasingly diverse sources to analyze and drive their operations, with those sources perhaps numbering in the thousands or millions. Enterprises are struggling with data's rise in terms of volume and variety. Data modernization addresses this key challenge and involves establishing a sturdy foundation of data by making it simple and accessible on the cloud. The following are the cloud adoption patterns IT is exploring as per the organization's business priority-

a. Cloud-Native: To build functional solutions quickly.
b. Cloud-First: To take advantage of the cloud without committing to migrating existing solutions.
c. Lift and Shift: To minimize on-premises infrastructure.
d. Offload an Economical, more secure, scalable, or efficient way of running existing infrastructure.
e. Incremental Change: To harness the new possibilities of the cloud for IT assets modernization.
f. Experimental: Start exploring the cloud without a strategic commitment.

It is always advisable to do the initial assessment before adopting the cloud. This involves consideration of multiple factors like financial assessment, security, compliance assessment, and product license assessment. The financial assessment includes a cost comparison of on-prem vs cloud. The cost includes saving for CAPEX (servers, storage, OS), OPEX (bandwidth, maintenance, backup), and spending on migration, governance, and service cost. The security and compliance assessment includes understanding the regulatory or contractual obligations to store data in specific jurisdictions. This covers the geographic location to store the data, explores options if the organization decides to retrieve all the data back from the Cloud, and whether the Cloud vendor offers options to download or delete the data. The product license assessment review ensures on-prem existing software licenses in the cloud. The benefits of the cloud make it easy for enterprises to cloud adoption but some of the aspects depend on how providers react to non-functional requirements, downtime, or data security as this will have a direct impact on business.

Business and IT are exploring options on "How to build state-of-the-art software without a big infrastructure and operations unit and major investments in hardware?". They are considering cloud-native applications as the way to move forward as it adapts quickly to changing surroundings, consumer preferences, regulatory demands, or technological changes investments in IT.

4.2 Cloud Native

According to the Cloud Native Computing Foundation, "Cloud native technologies empower organizations to build and run scalable applications in modern, dynamic environments such as public, private, and hybrid clouds". Cloud Native applications are different from cloud-enabled ones. The cloud-enabled applications are developed by using traditional software methodology and can deploy in the cloud without using all benefits of the cloud. Cloud-native is how software is designed and implemented in the cloud environment using Cloud Native software. Cloud-native approaches together the various technologies, processes, and services to produce an outcome that has actual business value. The objective is to improve the speed and efficiency of service assembly, enabling the business to react faster to market change.

Microservices, Containerization, and leveraging NoSQL databases are important in the phase of designing and developing MDM cloud-native applications. Microservices allow you to build a system that is composed of multiple subsystems whereas containerization allows you to configure the dependencies in a package. The critical element is the horizontally scalable nature where leveraging NoSQL database technology shows proven commitments in managing any volume of master data from legacy systems. NoSQL stores and retrieves data from multiple formats which include key-value stores, graph databases, column-family (Bigtable) stores, document stores, and even rows in tables. The cloud-native transformations include "greenfield" which means developing the application from scratch or "brownfield" which is the modernization of an existing application to achieve stages of maturity and advantage of modern cloud architectures such as containers, event-driven architecture, DevSecOps (development, security, and operations), microservices and serverless Architecture.

4.3 Cloud MDM

Technology is not a barrier for MDM on cloud adoption. It is more of a challenge to move the entire data management efforts to the cloud. One must remember, MDM is as much about application information governance, so unless those applications reside in the cloud, moving data outside of the firewall simply adds more complexity. Data management services offered via software as a service (SaaS) help some of the technical aspects of MDM, specifically of data quality services with the challenge of re-locating the business role of data stewardship from business users (behind the firewall) to "stewardship in the cloud".

We generally see two use cases in organizations having to start an MDM journey on the cloud. These are:

a. Move on-prem MDM to Cloud
b. Implementing new or re-platform MDM solutions on the cloud

For migrating an existing on-prem MDM implementation to the cloud, it is important to check with existing MDM vendors to understand the support and the cloud roadmap. The challenge is, as your data platform grows, you may find yourself in a situation where the existing toolset (ETL, MDM, BI, etc.) doesn't allow you to easily implement some needed business functionality and leaves us with only the choice to build a workaround. In our experience, these workarounds will become as complex as the initial solution itself and you will end up with what we fondly call a **"spaghetti architecture."** You will need to make sure the vendors have development and support plans for all the tools and technologies used in the current architecture on the cloud.

When implementing MDM on the cloud, you also need to look at different offerings that combine product capabilities with cloud management service levels. Major vendors are offering cloud-based solutions such as software as a service (SaaS), managed services, or licensed to run and manage by yourself on your cloud. Some vendors with traditional on-prem monolithic MDM solutions have ported their legacy MDM products to run on the cloud. They might have added some cloud-native capabilities, but these adapted legacy MDM applications are not the same as full-blown cloud-native MDM.

For new / re-platform MDM initiatives, considering Cloud Native MDM solutions is one of the options. The cloud-native pattern is built and runs completely on cloud infrastructure and services and adapts quickly to changing surroundings, consumer preferences, regulatory demands, or technological changes investments in IT. Cloud Native MDM solutions generally leverage microservices architecture and container technologies like Docker and Kubernetes with integrated Continuous Integration / Continuous Delivery (CI/CD) processes. This could be a multi-cloud approach by establishing one central cloud based IAM solution to have full control of access to computing.

Master data is considered a valued corporate asset and helps organizations leverage their information assets to strengthen competitive positions, drive business value, boost operational efficiencies, and more. The movement to the cloud is causing companies of all sizes and in all industries to think about how to keep business data that was previously secured inside a firewall safe and compliant as per industry and government regulations. The organization is ultimately responsible for its data and must have proper controls in place (or enabled through cloud vendors) to ensure the security and privacy of data. The CIA Triad (**C**onfidentiality, **I**ntegrity, and **A**vailability) is an information security model which guides an organization's efforts toward ensuring data security and controlling data in the cloud. **Confidentiality**, only authorized personnel with the appropriate privileges can access or have permission to modify certain data. **Integrity** maintains the trustworthiness of data by having it in the correct state and immune to any improper modifications. **Availability** means network resources are available to authorized users. CIA Triad principles are critical for data in the cloud environment. The agreements with the cloud vendors to eliminate the risk related to data stored on the same system as other organization's data, deleting data if decided to end a contract, data breaches, data location, etc. is a must for the cloud journey.

For MDM on the cloud, we must get clarity on the following from cloud providers before choosing the right partner for cloud strategy

a. Each country has its security and encryption requirements across industries like HIPAA (Health Insurance Portability and Accountability Act), Financial Industry regulatory authority (FINRA), Federal Information Security Management Act (FISMA), or PCI Security Standards (Payment Cards Industry).

Compliance with security is a must for each country's deployment.

b. NIST data destruction standard which covers clearing, purging, and destruction.

c. Control data access and data retention policies enforcement.

d. Data encryption to encrypt sensitive data (for example AES 256 standards or similar)

e. Performance, response time, and security for data in motion or rest must be independent of workloads

f. Choice between public, private cloud, or hybrid cloud

g. Possibility of development on the on-prem, non-cloud environment

The National Institute of Standards and Technology (NIST) is working on identifying gaps in cloud standards and specifications. It publishes gaps on its portal, thus providing opportunities for outside organizations to address the identified issues. Other organizations like Open Group, Open Cloud Consortium (OCC), or OASIS are also contributing to cloud standards.

MDM offerings become available as containerized solutions on Kubernetes platforms for private cloud consumption or as Software as a Service (SaaS) solutions on the public cloud or as a Native solution. This can be a major cultural shift for an organization that's used to having full control over its line-of-business applications. For reasons of corporate governance or compliance, many organizations are now realizing they need a cloud exit strategy, even for applications that run on global providers, such as Microsoft Azure, AWS, or Google Cloud. A business should form a clear cloud exit strategy during its initial cloud design and planning phases.

4.4 Integration Platform as a Service (iPaaS)

iPaaS solutions, deliver a cloud service for application, data, process, and service integration scenarios. iPaaS tools are cloud-based and provide platform support to application and data integration projects that involve cloud-to-cloud, cloud-to-on-premises, and on-premises-to-on-premises integration. For application-to-application integration, iPaaS tools are used to connect applications, systems, or data located on-premises or in the cloud, and automatically implement interfaces and data flows to establish and manage each integration. The microservices integration enables automatically generating and publishing APIs to support microservices. Data integration covers data format translations and validates real-time synchronized data, as an alternative to traditional script-driven batch data transfers. iPaaS tools provide a greater degree of agility and scalability and can be considered as an alternative to legacy ETL offerings.

The most common method for data integration stands for extract, transform, and load. ETL includes extraction of the required information from the identified systems supporting multiple file formats like RDBMS, XML, CSV, Fixed Width, JSON, etc. With the transform process, the aggregate data is analyzed and transformed into the required format using parsing, standardization, harmonization, and matching capabilities of the data quality technologies. Loading of data is the final stage where the transformed data is loaded into the target system (MDM in this case) maintaining the referential integrity and data consistency. We can alternatively use programming languages like Python to build our own ETL pipelines, but it is important to consider that there are benefits to using existing ETL tools over trying to build a data pipeline from scratch. ETL has been a critical part of IT infrastructure for years and covers most use cases and technical requirements. There is a significant difference between the ETL (extract, transform, load) approach and ELT (extract, load, transform) approach. With ELT, the data is extracted and loaded immediately to leverage the computing power of the target database and planned for transformations at a later stage. With the rise of cloud technologies and cloud data warehouses, the ELT pattern is advisable to consider massive parallel processing.

****

Chapter 5: Reference Architecture

To develop a successful data ecosystem in any organization, the most crucial part is how they design the data architecture and the understanding of the data life cycle which covers upstream and downstream systems, data storage, data latency, integration, and the critical aspects of an application such as availability, logging, maintainability, maintenance, networking, performance concerns, reliability, scalability, and security.

5.1 Layered Architecture

The most common architecture pattern in MDM is the layered architecture pattern, otherwise known as the n-tier architecture pattern. It is a set of interlinked components, services, processes, and interfaces organized into functional layers. Components within the layered architecture pattern are organized into horizontal layers, each layer performing a specific role within the application. Although the layered architecture pattern does not specify the number and types of layers that must exist in the pattern, MDM layered architecture is recommended to consist of six standard layers.

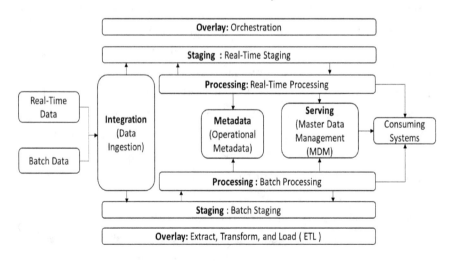

Figure 12 Layered Architecture

These layers are as follows.

a. Integration layer, for batch and real-time ingestion
b. Staging layer, data to be staged for data quality dimensions (optional)
c. Processing layer, for batch and real-time processing of data
d. Metadata layer to enhance our processing layer.
e. Serving layer – The MDM Solution
f. Overlay layer for ETL and/or orchestration.

Data Integration layer

Data integration in MDM is the process to extract critical data from various sources to achieve a unified view of it. This includes data from internal sources (line of business, shared service, or group function) and external sources. The integration (ingestion) layer connects to the source systems and brings data into the solution, preserving original data formats. The ingestion layer recommended considering three important aspects

a. Allows to add new connector types to accommodate new types of data sources
b. The movement of data should be visible. Should expose critical metrics, like data throughput and latency
c. The recommendation is to use different tools/processes for batch and real-time. This helps in eliminating dependency if there are directions to change the tools or process.

The data ingestion framework is the core of the architecture. It is advisable to build a metadata-driven framework to ingest the source systems data where you have just one pipeline that ingests multiple datasets. Getting data from multiple systems and developing one-on-one data pipelines would make it a maintenance headache. Metadata is described as the kind of data that gives more information about the data. In this context, metadata would be required to be stored in a data engineering metadata database and should describe the entire process of sourcing, which files from a certain system and the files belong to a certain dataset, and how they should be adjusted and stored in the database. The orchestration pipeline will have a responsibility to draw the ingestion information from the metadata therapies and then pass it onto the ingestion pipeline.

Organizations today have reached the maturity level where they in general know what they want from data integration, the type of data to be collected, where that data comes from, the participating systems, the frequency of data, and building master data models. The specific challenge the enterprises are having is to define the route to consolidating into the master environment, use the parsing, standardization, harmonization, and matching capabilities of the data quality technologies, and generate business intelligence out of it.

We observed two types of ingestion patterns for an MDM Solution, information-focused, and process-focused integration. The *Information focused pattern* deals with the building of an MDM Hub with an initial load of data as well as distributing master data to upstream and downstream systems. The value of this pattern is to load cleansed, standardized, de-duplicated master data aligned to architectural deliverables. It also covers bi-directional master data synchronization to maintain a single source of truth across all systems at any given point in time. *Process-focused integration* patterns deal with the integration of MDM and other application systems, with a focus on process capabilities. This pattern allows the authoring of master data in the application system while still getting all of the benefits from the MDM Hub.

Both patterns are application agnostic and can be combined and used as a composite pattern to address a particular business need. As an example, the customer onboarding process is to be integrated with MDM de-dup services to prevent duplicates or integrate publish/subscribe MDM features with business processes where master data-consuming applications need to be notified about master data changes.

Data Staging

The staging layer in reference architecture enables data availability for consumption in batch or real-time. As an example, frameworks that allow you to process data in real time (MQ, Kafka, and so on) are tied to the real-time staging layer. Batch staging is for your data ingested through Batch (ETL). Real-time staging is a message bus for data coming message by message. This layer is generally used by businesses to confirm the data available as per the data quality dimensions defined. The staging layer recommended considering three important aspects

a. Reliable should be able to persist data in the face of various failures.
b. Scalable, add extra storage capacity with minimal effort
c. Performance, read data with high enough throughput

Data Processing

This layer is the heart of the data platform where all the required business logic is applied, and all the data validations and data transformations take place. The layer is responsible for delivering data outputs to consumers, usually other systems. The distributed data processing engine is recommended for both batch and real-time.

Operational Metadata

Metadata-driven ETL framework reduces the dependency on vendor toolsets where adding new data sources may require complicated customization of code. The framework enables a flexible layer that simplifies the technology learning curve and reduces the time to implement new data sources. It involves creating templates for data migration controls, exception handling, and rules management. This layer includes schema information from data sources, statistics like processed row counts, the status of ingestion like success or failure, error handling logic, and job control parameters stored in configuration files to generate executable ETL jobs. The Metadata Driven Framework approach yields a uniform generic way of data ingestion which eliminates the inconsistency that is seen when different developers perform similar work. The code that results from the framework is standardized and easy to review and maintain. Any changes to ingestion mainly would consist of modifying the DMLs for meta-data without any code change. The Framework can be used to generate custom factory templates of XML which can be imported into vendor toolsets to generate ETL from the framework.

Data Consumers

Consumers are data stewards and downstream systems. Data access from staging allows data stewards to work directly with raw, unprocessed data to measure Data Quality dimensions and to build transformation and business rules for ETL. Data access from MDM systems allows systems to consume organized master data

Orchestration and ETL layers

These layers are responsible for managing multiple data processing jobs. This is where data gains its "intelligence", as logic is applied to transform the data from a transactional nature to an analytical nature. The responsibility of these layers is spread across many different tools. The tools are typically classified as data-integration tools and are used to extract data from multiple data sources, transform the data to a required target structure, and load the data into the target datastore. Both layers can generate and use metadata definitions for data attributes and entities. It also includes components that perform data consistency and data quality analysis as well

5.1.1 Change Data Capture

For a successful master data management initiative, businesses need to have timely access to changed data in source systems. Change Data Capture technology quickly identifies and processes only the data that has changed and provides feeds to MDM projects. When it comes to choosing the right CDC method, the requirements for capturing changes and the purpose of data in the target system are important to realize. For example, some applications may need changes on a table-by-table basis, while others may want the changes based on units of work (i.e., across multiple tables). The CDC is broadly classified as synchronous and asynchronous. The synchronous CDC is based on triggers on the source database and captured as part of the transaction modifying the source table. The asynchronous CDC covers timestamp, snapshot, and log-based techniques. The timestamp-based technique extracts the change data sets based on the timestamp field in the source. The snapshot-based technique extracts the change data sets by comparing incremental snapshots with the initial source snapshot. Log Based Technique depends on database transaction log files that record every DML operation (write, delete, and update events) along with the timestamp to spot the changes and perform CDC operations. When choosing a CDC solution, a key architectural consideration is the ease of interoperability with its current implementation. All CDC solutions have a certain degree of system impact which needs to be evaluated before starting the design.

5.1.2 Master Data Synchronization

The MDM implementation comes with the mechanics of parsing, standardization, corrections, consolidation, and merging. It is one of the needs for business application owners to have access to consistent data across all systems. Data synchronization is the process of keeping the critical data assets the same between MDM and the contributing systems. This can be done in real-time, in near real-time, or batches depending upon the business needs and an underlying architecture style. The MDM products in the market today generally provide configurable frameworks that define and send critical data entities to multiple applications if there is a change event. The interested systems can subscribe to messages for consumption. For legacy systems, which do not support publish-subscribe architecture, a separate layer is recommended for source system-specific consumption rather than customizing the MDM solution to source specific.

5.1.3 Microservices and SOA

Both microservices architecture and SOA are considered service-based architectures (distributed architecture). There is common faith to develop software components with standard application programming interfaces (APIs), using common services and managed through orchestration, middleware, integration methods, and management tools. Microservices are deployed as autonomous services functions, simpler to construct and deploy compared to monolithic applications or service-oriented architectures (SOAs). The services are deployed as packaged business capabilities and are adopted by organizations where each piece can be developed and maintained by multiple agile teams in short development sprints to achieve the speed and flexibility expected from the master data management (MDM) systems. The microservices layer enables the MDM APIs to decompose monolithic MDM processes, and accommodate flexibility and rapid change in the MDM changing circumstances without compromising business value.

5.1.4 Enterprise Identifier Concept

The concept of enterprise identifier is an integral part of master data management practices. In the consolidated style of master data management, where a single, master view of a party is maintained, the enterprise identifier plays a vital role in ensuring that you can get a true understanding of what constitutes a party.

An enterprise identifier is simply a globally unique identifier that is assigned to a party when the party is introduced into an organization. That identifier remains with the party throughout its life cycle. All the systems in which a party is kept agree on this identifier. Using enterprise identifier, the organization can know with confidence that "John Smith" in System A is the same "John Smith" in System B without having to carry out a great deal of auxiliary processing such as ensuring that addresses are also the same, that the date of birth is the same.

5.2 MDM Reimagination

MDM is a discipline essential to obtaining a trusted 360° view of master data which helps many critical operational processes such as consistent customer experience, cross-sell, and up-sell, in a multichannel architecture, or streamlined new product introduction. Companies have now started taking advantage of the information on social media, Blogs, Twitter, Facebook, and other sources of public data. Data is becoming the world's new natural resource and companies are now forced to rethink traditional MDM methods. The willingness of consumers to create public data on themselves helps companies to know their customers better. With IoT gaining momentum, the evolution of "smart" and "sensing" devices will drive an exponential increase in data volumes and access methods. Integration with a social network, providing real-time information, and applying artificial intelligence to solve critical issues around speed and scale will drive next-generation MDM.

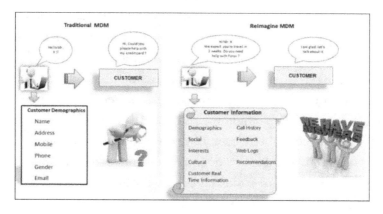

Figure 13 NextGen MDM

An emerging trend next to MDM is the rise of the concepts of the digital twin and customer data platform (CDP), which is a new software segment next to MDM that is in the Gartner Hype Cycle for technologies currently at the peak of inflated expectations. The new insights from external sources into MDM allow organizations to improve customer relationships and service through a deeper understanding of their customers. People provide a wealth of information through social media about their preferences, interests, the people they follow, and the product they rate.

The important aspect is "Which data should be included". Insights from social data enter into personal areas, like health, status, or financial well-being. Human communication is personal; so are insights. The data from Twitter and Facebook could help to predict credit ratings. There are projects to scan social networks for information that could lead to conclusions about a person's financial capacity. There is resistance from people that this is like spying on your citizens, but it all depends on what you do with the data. In short, many data sources are sensitive, including social media data. While collecting the data, we need to see how best to use the data.

5.2.1 The shift from Relational to NoSQL

As part of the Information Management strategy, various Data initiatives need to be executed within an organization at the business and enterprise level. All such initiatives need a data mindset at both strategic and operational execution levels. Increased data volumes in organizations require a solid foundation in data architecture. The organization usually uses a combination of several types of databases to meet business data requirements other than big data requirements. It can be a relational database or non-relational databases (NoSQL) databases. SQL database function mostly handles structured data, which is in the form of rows and columns while the NoSQL database function ranges from semi-structured to unstructured data.

The SQL databases are further classified as OLTP databases (online transactional processing) and OLAP databases (online analytical processing). OLTP systems prefer normalized tables to avoid data redundancy while improving data integrity and consistency of their business data. MDM is an OLTP system (Online Transaction Processing), consisting of ACID-compliant transactions. ACID compliance is an industry term that covers the Atomicity,

Consistency, Isolation, and Durability of transactions. As an example, **Atomicity** means, if you are making a transaction, it either happens or does not happen at all. There is no partial success. **Consistency** means that data must follow defined rules of the database, and these rules can vary from data validation rules such as null data checks, unique checks, or even primary key checks when a transaction doesn't follow these rules. It will be rolled back to its previous state. **Isolation** means that all transactions happen in isolation, and they do not affect one another. **Durability** means successful transactions will be saved in the system and when there is a system failure, the transaction must persist. One thing to note here is most modern web apps produce JSON Data Type, which is an unstructured data type. OLTP systems prefer structured data and there will be transformation to convert unstructured JSON data into rows and columns. OLAP systems are optimized for running analytical queries and doing data aggregation across a large amount of data. OLAP systems tend to have more than one database for reporting organized in the form of facts and dimensions. OLAP systems are ideal for data warehousing where data from various other sources allow business intelligence tools to create impactful business reports, which enable businesses to view KPI reports or make critical decisions. The MDM 360 views of data and business intelligence report power critical business decision-making processes.

NoSQL databases are designed to handle large volumes of distributed data. The flexibility and the schema design make NoSQL databases a great option for building modern applications. The goal of NoSQL databases is not to replace SQL or relational databases but to work together. In the dynamic business requirements world, most of the time SQL and NoSQL databases are integrated to handle various business challenges. The NoSQL database handles various data formats, such as unstructured data, and semi-structured data allowing the high velocity of data and can horizontally be scalable by partitioning. We have different types of NoSQL databases for different use cases. It can be in the form of key values, stored documents, databases, white columns, databases, graph databases, or even search engines. The examples of popular NoSQL database technology are as below)

a. Apache HBase - Wide-column NoSQL database
b. AWS DynamoDB - fully managed proprietary NoSQL database service that supports key–value and document data structures
c. Cassandra - open-source, distributed, wide-column store, NoSQL database management system designed to manage large amounts of data across many commodity servers, providing high availability with no single point of failure
d. CouchDB - Document-based NoSQL database
e. Elasticsearch - Elasticsearch is a document-oriented database. Highly scalable, full-text search and analytics engine for real-time searching, storing, and analyzing huge volumes of data
f. Google Bigtable – high-performance NoSQL database service for large analytical and operational workloads.
g. MarkLogic - MarkLogic is a multi-model NoSQL database that has evolved from its XML database roots to also store JSON documents and RDF triples natively for its semantic data model. It uses a distributed architecture that can handle hundreds of billions of documents and hundreds of terabytes of data.

5.3 Semantic MDM

Some of the emerging technologies in the data storing realm are presenting new ways of solving the challenges we have with data quality and traditional entity-relationship-based data models. As data practitioners, many of us work mainly on the data supply side. Our mission is to derive value from data. We collect and generate data, we represent, integrate, store, and make it accessible through data models for usage and exploitation to build predictive, descriptive, or analytics solutions. This mission is often compromised when the data models of the supply side are misunderstood and misused by the exploitation side, and/or when the data requirements of the exploitation side are misunderstood by the supply side. In both cases, the problem is caused by insufficient or problematic modeling of the data's semantics. This gap is the semantic gap and hence the need for Semantic data models arises.

Organizations would want a semantic model to standardize and align the meaning of typically heterogeneous and managed-in-silos data, provide it with context, and make it more discoverable, interoperable, and usable for analytics and other purposes. Semantic data models cover defining descriptions and representations of data that are more explicit, accurate, and commonly understood by both humans and computer systems. The data artifacts include metadata schemas, controlled vocabularies, taxonomies, ontologies, knowledge graphs, entity-relationship (E-R) models, property graphs, and other conceptual models for data representation. Applying graph theory to Master Data Management initiatives provides better insights. Graph Databases, as a technology with object-oriented concepts with nodes and edges (relationships), map very well to the master data domains (party, account, product, location) and the relationships. The value of Graph Databases lies in their ability to complement your MDM and data governance applications. Organizing master data in a graph offers a proven approach to solving data challenges, yields relevant answers faster with more flexibility to solve pressing problems, and creates immediate business value. As organizations continue to look for new technologies and the next best action to improve customer experience, the notion of a semantic model to master data has evolved. Semantic data models cover defining descriptions and representations of data more explicitly, accurately, and commonly understood. The data artifacts include metadata schemas, controlled vocabularies, taxonomies, ontologies, knowledge graphs, entity-relationship (E-R) models, property graphs, and other conceptual models for data representation. Having the ontologies and data in a graph database to form a knowledge graph does help in facilitating deep learning using machine learning tools.

Semantic is great for providing meaning, looking up facts, describing relationships between entities, and exploring those relationships, including the ability to traverse them as well as infer new facts. Semantic is being used for a wide range of applications, from dynamic publishing to providing recommendations to intelligence discovery to metadata management to integrating data from silos. Google search interface uses semantics, for populating their knowledge panel, displayed when there is semantic data available for what was entered into the search. Google claims their knowledge graph allowed searching for things, not strings

The universal framework for semantics is called the Resource Description Framework (RDF), a standard for modeling data that uses three simple components: a subject, predicate, and object. Triple stores semantic facts in the form of subject–predicate–object using the Resource Description Framework. Triple stores are not a replacement for relational databases. In practical scenarios, they are used in conjunction with relational databases enabling smart integration of data using intelligent Metadata to describe the core information. Discovering, understanding, and utilizing relationships between and among people and organizations are key elements of Semantic MDM systems. Current MDM systems support direct relationships, hierarchical relationships, and the grouping of parties. For example, we know that the customer opens an account. We have another fact that Account is related to Product. We can infer a new fact: Customers bought products. Semantics makes such relationships all have meaning, and that meaning will always stay intact and can be leveraged, as you integrate data from different systems.

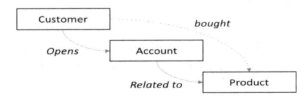

Semantic technologies are very powerful, and can be very useful, but

also require care and understanding. We see great promise in these technologies, but it is more for extending and enriching existing MDM architectures than replacing them. The Chief Data Officers organization looking to leverage a semantic layer solution to make data, models, and analysis more accessible, consistent, and secure across the organization.

5.3.1 Implementation View – Examples

Information View

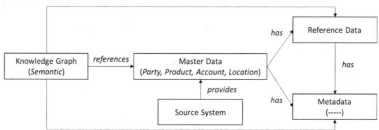

Figure 14 Implementation View with Master Data

Sample Graph View

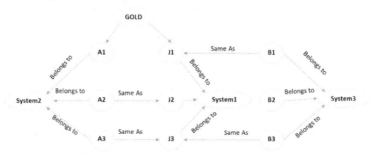

Figure 15 Graph representation of sample data

5.4 Data as a Service (DaaS Framework)

Data has always been considered necessary for the core operations of running a business. The latest popular wave of on-demand services is Data as a Service (DaaS) which is defined as a framework for designing and developing a set of reusable data services based on enterprise-level standards

The Data Service Layer makes it possible to use real-time analytics as part of your everyday processes, taking advantage of knowledge buried in unstructured information, and providing real-time access to aggregated cleansed information. The layer is built to centralize data and metadata access, security management, and provide platform neutrality and abstraction from data complexity. Some organizations deploy data services based solely on an SOA solution with no data integration, governance, or master data management (MDM) strategy in place. This makes the overall solution untenable for enterprise usage. The DaaS framework entails a paradigm shift that helps organizations to transform themselves into data-driven organizations.

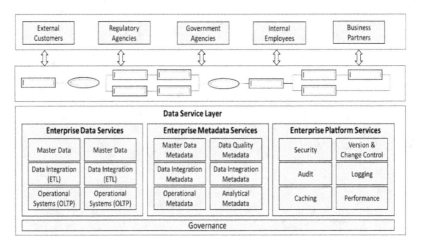

Figure 16 Data as a Service Framework

DaaS is an architectural framework and not merely a technology or an application. This enables end users the capability to have access to data from multiple sources by leveraging reusable data services that meet enterprise and industry-wide standards. Building enterprise-level data services may require changes in enterprise-level policies and standards to ensure a consistent operating model across all divisions. The purpose of governance is to transform this by streamlining the information flow and major business services and processes within the extended enterprise.

5.5 Data Security and Protection

Introducing MDM in an enterprise creates a paradox. On one side of the coin, the value of the master data is significantly improved by having it with a high-quality, managed, and centralized system, enabling a business to see master data instances with a 360-degree view. However, on the flip side of the coin, integrated data platforms are attractive targets for unauthorized access subject to information security risks. Data protection is a business imperative and is critical for all organizations. This covers controlled access to sensitive data and preferably protects the sensitive data using encryption. Organizations must address data privacy as a design time attribute to ensure privacy by default.

The MDM programs are aligned with data protection initiatives, maintaining accurate master data representation, understanding and classifying the personal information, what all constitutes, Personally Identifiable Information (PII) and Sensitive Personal Information (SPI), and then controlling the flow of data as well as demarcating the boundaries around the same by combining people, process, data, and technology. The risk of master data compromise includes compliance risk, reputational risks, strategic risks, and transactional risks with numerous government and industry regulations and laws.

Compliance (legal) risk

Unauthorized disclosure of PII (personally identifiable information) could expose an organization to litigation and financial penalties. PII standards are based on Industry data protection standards which cover Payment Card Industry Data Security Standards (PCI DSS) or Health Insurance Portability and Accountability Act (HIPAA) and Geographical data protection standards cover General Data Protection Regulation (GDPR) and the ePrivacy Directive (ePR) as an example

Reputational & Strategic risk

Information security breaches and failure to maintain accurate business information impact the organization's growth plan, strategic decisions, the reputation of the business, and customer confidence.

Transaction risk

Transaction risk may arise from fraud, error, or inappropriate business processes, people, and systems covering areas such as customer service, systems development and support, internal control processes, and capacity planning. Transaction risk may affect other risk types such as contractual risk, disaster risk, or other business risks.

5.5.1 Regulatory Drivers for Data Protection

Concerns over confidential data in general and customer data privacy and data security have resulted in a broad range of legislative and regulatory requirements for data security. There are data protection legalization initiatives across the globe like GDPR (Global data protection and Regulation) in Europe, PIPEDA (Canada), PDPB (India), NDB (Australia), CCPA (California), and the evolving data privacy laws in North America enforcing the privacy rights of customer and individuals. The Sarbanes-Oxley Act (SOX) mandates knowledge of who has access to what information and that proper security controls are in place to ensure data confidentiality and integrity.

Privacy in MDM is an orthogonal concern to security and is focused on the appropriate use of personal data based on regulation and the explicit consent of the party. The MDM architecture must be flexible to accommodate regulatory requirements for multi-country implementation. Assessing compliance requirements and applying the appropriate controls will be an ongoing effort to align with the latest regulatory mandates. The final goal is to ensure that data protection is considered part of architecture and that privacy should be an integrated part of the MDM solution

5.5.2 Principals of Privacy by Design

a. People aspect covers Awareness, Training, Roadshows, and Data Culture with respect for privacy

b. The process covers Transparency, Lawfulness, and Rights of Individuals,

c. Data covers building architecture and standards with privacy by Design, Interoperability, and Open Standards

d. Technology aspects cover Vulnerability, Patching and Hardening, Cryptography, and Specialized tools.

e. Data Governance capabilities

f. Data Lineage and Data Classification capabilities

g. Restrict data collection criteria

h. Authorized access to data and review security aspects for all touchpoints

i. Data Archival policies

j. The cultural shift in making people held responsible for any security violation

k. Mandating Audit Trail as core capability

l. Data Encryption capabilities

m. Apply algorithms to detect infringements at the earliest and notify impacted customers and the regulators

n. Periodically revisit and update Data Privacy Policy and notify stakeholders accordingly.

5.5.3 Data Security Directives

The data security directives cover the aspects of understanding the potential risks to your master data, visualizing where the vulnerabilities and associated threats are, and applying the appropriate controls to address those risks. This comprises (i) Identity and access management, authentication, and authorization for the usage of MDM applications (ii) Services and data requirements for security, privacy, and confidentiality of the information, and (iii) Information technology architecture and infrastructure implications of developing and deploying secure and integrated MDM solutions.

Access and Authorization - This directive enforces the permissions stated in the user authorization policy regarding what information and computing resources the authenticated party is allowed to access. This allows you to control who sees what, who can add persistent data, and grant access to a resource based on identity. The directive uses role-based access control, and every role must have an assigned owner

Accountability - Individual accountability to breach security policy is monitored as a time-stamped log of events.

Audit -This directive enforces all sensitive transactions and events of user accounts that must be logged. A "golden thread" must be maintained in such a way that all audit events can be traced back to the origin. Auditing is used to reconstruct who did what after the fact.

Authentication - This directive is a verification component to verify that an individual or a party is whom they claim they are.

Confidentiality - Process and policy enforced to protect information from unauthorized use.

Integrity - Deals with accidental or malicious changes to data

User Management - This directive covers the process of defining, creating, maintaining, and deleting user authorizations or the authorized privilege. It enforces that the Information is modified or disclosed to only authorized users. Active Directory will be used to authenticate users. Typically, this is an LDAP directory in an enterprise.

5.5.4 MDM Solution Security Approach

Enterprises in the MDM journey needs to protect integrated data from the compromise of unauthorized access and use. Businesses can no longer afford to ignore MDM server security as a foundational requirement. A well-defined Data Policy overarching the ethical, legal, and regulatory parts is a must for all organizations. There are two foundations of MDM functional security requirements

Securing the request with authentication and authorization

The authentication is managed by Application Server where authenticated users are given a "Service Consumers" role. The authorization is handled by the MDM server application where all security policies are configured in the MDM database or in a repository

Controlling the visibility and accessibility of data.

The functionality of setting up the control of who sees what and who can add persistent data using data-level entitlements is to be developed, customized, or configured in MDM solutions. This foundation requirement must safeguard both Data at Rest and Data in Motion. As a business non-functional requirement, all security management events are to be logged. This includes changes in system configuration, changes in user privileges, changes in management tasks, or security administration. This also covers firewall, VPN, encryption, intrusion detection, intrusion prevention, and vulnerability assessment.

Access to MDM data and functionality is controlled both at the application server level and at the application level. To invoke an MDM service, the following actions are performed

a. The system user authenticates the end user
b. The system user connects to the MDM.
c. The application server authenticates the system user.
d. MDM performs transaction access control using end-user credentials
e. MDM performs data access control using end-user credentials

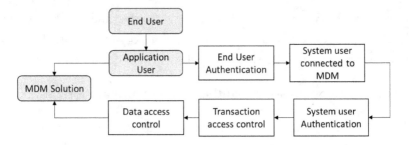

Figure 17 MDM Security Flow

All business operations carry some element of Risk. It is impossible to eliminate risk but with a proper mitigation plan, the risk can be reduced to a level that the organization can live with.

****

Chapter 6: Infusing AI into MDM

The manual nature and time and money investment of integrating data sources in traditional MDM pose a big threat to speed and scalability. With the increasing volume of data sources, the speed of integration is related to the business value provided. AI as a technology is evolving every day and we are seeing an increase in all Industry sectors. The study from different research forums including Forrester, IDC, and Narrative Science, shows that there is a significant increase in investment in AI methodology to help improve customer experience and support executive productivity improvement. The examples of use cases from industries leveraging AI are

a. Banking and financial services: fraud prevention as ai learns what types of transactions are fraudulent, credit decisions, client segmentation
b. Communications, media, and technology: emotion analysis, real-time translation, automated journalism, content analysis for the organization, data analysis
c. Consumer goods & distribution: personalized communications, predictive supply chain
d. Education: automated grading, adaptive grading, customized digital learning interfaces, plagiarism checkers
e. Energy, resources, and utilities: market analysis, sales bots, client segmentation, robotics
f. Hi-tech: voice-to-text, smart personal assistant, client segmentation, photodetection, gesture control, facial recognition
g. Insurance: risk identification, personalized pricing, client support
h. Life sciences and healthcare: surgical robots, drug discovery, candidates for clinical trials, epidemic outbreak prediction, health monitoring, virtual doctors, automation of routine tasks like x-ray, CT scans, data entry
i. Manufacturing: weather detection, predictive analysis for environmental impacts, targeted advertising, market analysis,

client segmentation, unmanned aerial vehicles, wargaming, diagnosis and maintenance of weapons systems, civilian detection, sales bots

j. Public services: targeted campaigning, public opinion monitoring, anticipating infrastructure failures, and maintenance

k. Retail: cashless stores, virtual mirrors, footfall analysis, and store optimization

l. Travel, transportation, and hospitality: reducing travel times through analyzing traffic, ridesharing apps to determine the price and supply chain prediction, autonomous vehicles, smart hotel rooms, ai concierge

Leveraging AI and machine learning algorithms to automate the integration process empowers companies to get hold of the volume and variety of data sources. Machine learning algorithms like pattern detection, which automate new data source mapping to target, fix data quality, discover hidden relationships, and identify similarity in data help companies to solve critical issues around speed and scale in increasingly larger and more complex environments.

With our experience, we see three AI use cases for Master Data Management solutions

a. Using AI to simplify MDM configuration
b. Using AI capabilities within the matching engine
c. Using AI capabilities to significantly reduce the work for data stewards

6.1 AI to Simplify MDM Configuration

The initial load of data sources or adding more data sources in deployment phases is a complex process. The tasks include manual steps and many switches between disjoint data profiling tools, data governance catalog tools, and Microsoft Excel which is often used for the source to MDM mappings that cannot be substantially shortened either via additional resources or via traditional ETL-based approaches. As a result, the time to value is not ideal. The AI-infused capability in MDM configuration is associated with leveraging AI to extract and propose new business terms from Regulations, for example, GDPR, POPI, and BCBS 239 followed by the registration process of a new data source into a data governance catalog.

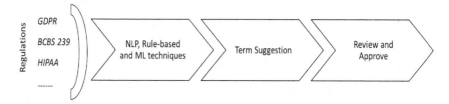

Figure 18 AI to suggest new business terms

NLP, Rule-based, and ML techniques are used to derive new business terms by identification, and tokenization to extract the relevant features for ML models. Data Steward can review and approve the proposed business terms or make corrections as necessary based on organization terminology. A similar pattern would be leveraged for auto-discovery of metadata, auto-analyze data quality, auto-detect sensitive data such as PII, auto-classify data, and auto-assign business terms.

Figure 19 AI-Infused Registration of a New Data Source

MDM system also acts as a data source and all attributes, data classes, and business terms are assigned. The data classification results of the MDM data model are compared to the data classes assigned to the source data model and mapping is proposed as a perfect match or a suggestion is made for the data analyst to review. A previously lengthy and time-consuming series of manual steps have now been automated to mostly a manual review.

6.2 AI-driven Matching Engine Capabilities

AI-driven matching engine uses a blend of probabilistic, linguistic, heuristic, and/or phonetic matching algorithms to automatically propose an initial set of weights to score the comparison results as well as an initial set of thresholds for the lower and upper thresholds, setting the boundaries for non-match, clerical, and auto-match results. Many MDM solutions use graph capabilities as part of the solution stack. While fuzzy probabilistic matching is certainly a very powerful technique to determine duplicates, graph neural networks (GNN) help in use cases to find hidden relationships which are not explicitly declared in MDM.

6.3 AI-driven Data Stewardship

AI-infused data stewardship for MDM provides capabilities to limit the number of clerical tasks the data stewardship team needs to process. The key idea is that an ML algorithm is used to learn from the data steward and their decisions while processing the duplicate suspect tasks. The trained AI model is deployed resolving most of the future tasks automatically. There are many kinds of Data Stewards, such as Business Data Stewards, Technical Data Stewards, Project Data Stewards, Domain Data Stewards, and Operational Data Stewards. Each has a role to play, and Data Stewards need to work together to achieve the desired results.

****

Chapter 7: Model-Driven Development

Solutions in the field of master data management tend to be complex in nature and revolve around business domains. A common mistake in building an MDM model is to consider it entirely as an extension of a database management system (DBMS) and ignore the business processes that are tightly coupled with the data models on which they operate. The goal of model-driven development is to describe master data-related processes for consistency and completeness and represent each of these processes as a model. A *model* represents the abstraction and a sufficient description of the problem domain. The approach focuses on the business domain, the issues, and behavior that revolve around that domain, and how this approach leads to a functioning system. A model-driven project requires more skilled designers than developers because source code and documentation are generated automatically from models

The diagram below illustrates model-driven development. The domain model describes the business supported by a business glossary, the life cycle, and rules. Business processes and use cases effectively control the data.

Domain Model

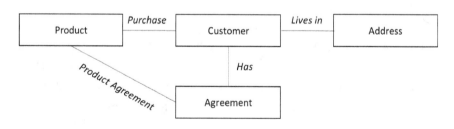

Business Glossary | Rules | Data Life Cycle | Business Services

The Business Service integration layer works on domain objects supporting business processes

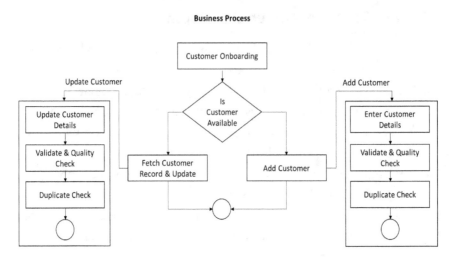

Figure 20 Model-driven approach

7.1 MDM Data Modeling

Master Data Management solution plays a significant role to enable in the organization a data-driven organization. It is a multi-faceted discipline that covers a wide range of subject areas from data quality to data governance, representing strategic and a single integrated definition of data, unbiased of any system or application. It is only within the context of a specific industry that an MDM data model should be developed to address the unique requirements of a business operating in that industry.

The master data model may include one or more master data domains such as Party, Product, Location, and Arrangement. Before building a model, it pays to enumerate and agree on the stakeholders and boundaries of the model. It is a good idea to limit the scope and set boundaries for the initial model.

The below diagram illustrates the key steps to model the MDM solution-

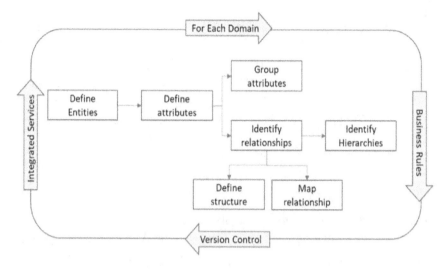

Figure 21 Design steps for the MDM data model

MDM model is an integrated view of the data produced and consumed across an entire organization which provides a "single version of the truth" focus on a specific industry/domain, minimizes data redundancy, disparity, and errors, core to data quality, consistency, and accuracy. It is different from the 3NF data modeling process. The 3NF modeling process does not divide the attributes into those that will be used for matching, entity resolution, and relationship resolution and those that will not be used for these purposes. In the MDM world, an MDM-Star schema is a natural representation of the concept of a master entity. The direction of one-to-many relationships from the center of the star to the attributes makes the MDM-Star look different from a data warehousing star schema structure, where one-to-many relationships are directed from the dimensions to the center of the star (fact table).

The model below represents an MDM-Star with an entity Customer that can have multiple names, multiple addresses, and multiple pieces of identification-

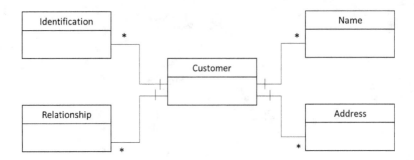

Figure 22 MDM Star for Customer Entity

The MDM model below enables the creation of relationships between the centers of the stars. It represents four entities (Individual, Account, and Organization) supported as relationship tables.

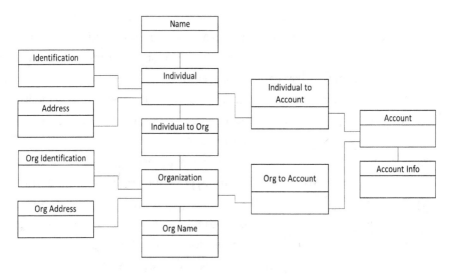

Figure 23 MDM Star with multiple entities

Time to market and the ability to integrate the efforts of multiple parties with diverse needs is the foundation upon which the ROI of the best-practice enterprise model is initially measured. A master data model must be designed to meet use cases such as entity resolution, relationship resolution, fast searches, flexibility to support multiple data domains and support consuming applications such as data warehouses, data marts, operational data stores, and so on. The model should also integrate with the data models of related industry models upon common data domains.

7.2 Canonical Models

Enterprise service framework enables data sharing and interoperability across systems to deliver SOA business services. SOA promises to help break down the silos of information across an organization and make it more consistent and available. It is important to define a common vocabulary (or set of semantics) for information across the enterprise and adopt a single canonical model to ensure data interoperability for data in motion. Many organizations are keen to accelerate this effort by adopting industry canonical schemas like Acord, FPML, Hl7, IFX, or reference models like Oracle AIA and IBM FSDM or IAA. These standards facilitate purposes such as the exchange of information between the various players within these industries and their value-chain members, data definitions for ongoing operations, and document specifications.

Use cases to opt for Canonical Data Model

The objective of working with a canonical model is to achieve consistency of data in motion across the enterprise integration stack. Designing a canonical data model is the first step to resolving cases of semantic conflict between applications. For example, packaged applications may represent the customer as a party and businesses are considering the party as a customer, a payer, or contact". These standards and frameworks use XML schema to create information models for the given use cases. If a new application is added to the integration solution or an existing application is likely to be replaced, the only transformation between the canonical data model is to be created or replaced.

Below are the use cases to opt for Canonical Data Model

a. How to manage the mandatory and optional of an entity in an MDM service contract? E.g., one of the services requires an element as mandatory and another service requires an optional

b. Reducing the impact of change. Any change in MDM canonical model, even if it is a single attribute change, it requires a rebuild of the services

c. Appropriate schema level validations and enumerations.

d. Redefining the canonical elements in the service contract. When a business scenario does not need the whole set of attributes that is available in the MDM service contract

e. Decoupling application-specific business objects and generic business objects

The canonical data model provides an additional level of indirection between applications' data formats, and it is important to design when to opt for the canonical data model. While it is important to design a more maintainable solution, canonical data models introduce additional latency in the flow of messages. Each message must undergo two translation steps, translation from the source application format into the common format and from the common format into the target application format. It is also advisable to design the model with only the portion of data that participates in messaging rather than the complete set of data within the application(s) to reduce message complexity. For very high throughput systems with performance requirements, direct translation may be the only choice.

The canonical model is to be developed domain-wise in alignment with the underlying Enterprise Data Model (EDM) and close partnership with business stewards for data exchange and interoperability aligned. Enterprise Data Model and the Canonical model should go hand-in-hand. The enterprise data model (EDM) is data-centric and represents the state of persistent entities (data) and their relationships.

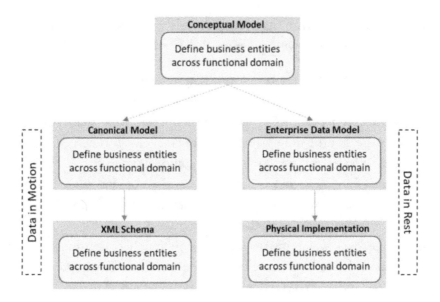

Figure 24 Enterprise and Canonical Model

The canonical model is application-centric and represents a standardized and consistent way of representing data in a common business language. In the absence of an EDM, the IT organization can struggle to understand what the impact is of extending or modifying some of the data services to meet new business requirements or newly introduced government regulations. Developing a canonical model helps harmonize shared information and results in a more efficient development process. This model-based approach includes the process of identifying, modeling, and documenting data requirements from the top (Business) to the bottom (implementations). This will result in more consistent and usable standards. The canonical model approach also enables leveraging common ESB services based on common data definitions. The common ESB services include business-level logging, auditing, and event-based visibility. The common model also supports business process orchestration simplification as processes operate within a single consistent data format.

Business Problem with Canonical Models

Based on experience with different clients, the common argument is -

a. Industry models are billed as a handy shortcut, but prebuilt data models are more trouble than they are worth.
b. Industry data models are an appealing concept at first blush, but they are not the time savers they are cracked up to be.
c. The vocabulary used by the operational source system's data model anyhow needs to be translated into the business vernacular. Embracing an industry-standard model introduces the need for yet another pocket dictionary.
d. Some data will translate without too much compromise; other data will need to be wrestled and coerced into a pre-defined model and invariably some source data just won't fit.
e. The challenges surrounding the translations between three languages-source systems, industry model, and business usage, is the opportunity to lose something.
f. ETL processing time frames, or data staging windows, are typically small, and a lot of time is required to run the transformation.

Best practice to leverage Canonical Models

The best practice to leverage industry data models are

a. Focus on usage. We should use a usage-centered approach to development driven by use cases or usage scenarios, not a data-centered one driven by data models. Data is an important part of the overall picture, but if we focus on data and not usage, we run the risk of building something that nobody is interested in using.
b. Prove the architecture early. Everything works in PowerPoint slides, on a whiteboard, or in CASE tool models but it isn't until you prove it with code that your architecture works. It is recommended that you build a working, end-to-end "skeleton" of your system to prove that all aspects of it work. This would entail that you show that you can access the major legacy data sources,

that your extract-transform-load (ETL) strategy works, that your database regression testing strategy works, and that your reporting tools can access your DW.

c. A common mistake which often leads to failure is to let technology decisions drive your prioritization strategies. The fundamental problem is that technical prioritization strategies do not reflect the priorities of the business which you are trying to support, putting any IT effort at risk because your stakeholders aren't receiving concrete value in a timely manner. When stakeholders don't perceive the value that they're getting for their IT investment they quickly start to rethink such investment.

d. Don't get hung up on "the one truth". The "one truth" philosophy says that it is desirable to have a single definition for a data element or business term. The fact is that various portions of your organization have different ways of working, different priorities, and different constraints. Seeking the one truth for a data element often proves to be an artificial constraint imposed by traditional data professionals, not by the actual business.

e. Active stakeholder participation. Stakeholder involvement is critical throughout your project, and better yet active stakeholder participation is where stakeholders are not only involved with your project on a daily basis, but they are also directly involved with the actual modeling effort itself

f. Having Analytics May Not Be Enough. Organizations can turn raw data into information through data warehouses and reporting interfaces but might fail in providing actual decision-making on time. Organizations need to improve business intelligence and decision-making through guided, predictive analytics which focuses on modeling to create competitive advantages.

Canonical Models – Examples

Integration in the Financial Enterprise – IFX Model

The Interactive Financial Exchange Business Message Specification (IFX) is designed for use in the financial services industry. The IFX specification represents a standard for business-to-business communications between financial organizations, third-party suppliers of services, and their customers. IFX is not based on an enterprise-wide model and is designed as a message standard. Organizations considering a message-based architecture are faced with the problem of selecting an appropriate set of messages to support their existing and future applications. This is where Industry standard models like IBM IFW Object Models come into the picture.

The IBM IFW offering is based on an enterprise-wide model of the financial organization, that includes 80% of the business concepts and functions needed by a financial organization. The IFW models support the expression of a financial organization's enterprise-wide needs in the BOM (Business Object Model) and a corresponding component and interface model in the IDM (Interface Design Model).

Integration in the Insurance Enterprise – ACORD Framework

ACORD Framework is a series of interrelated models to define the nature of the Insurance Industry. There are five parts or facets to the ACORD Framework. Each facet has one or more relationships with others, and they collectively represent different views of the business of insurance

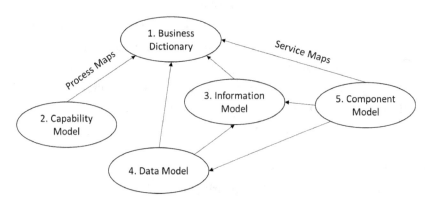

Figure 25 Acord Framework

Business Dictionary - It consists of insurance concepts (such as

Party, Claim) definitions, domain usages, and references. The main idea is to standardize the terms with teams to ensure terms are used synonymously across the models

Capability Model - The capability model allows the functional decomposition in areas such as Claims, Parties, Business Activity Management, and Services. The process maps list the important processes within a given capability.

Data Model – The data model is a logical-level entity-relationship model aligned to Information Model

Component Model – This model organizes data and behavior into components, and contains the logical groupings along with service maps, which are the interface definitions of those components.

Information Model - The model defines a conceptual overview of the entire industry as UML. The model contains many functional areas, including Agreement (i.e., policies and non-policy contracts), Product, Party (i.e., people and organizations), and Claims. Below are the industry-wise examples

Industry	Canonical Scheme
Insurance	ACORD http://www.acord.org
Banking	FpML http://www.fpml.org
Healthcare	HL7 http://www.hl7.org
Financial Exchange	IFX http://www.ifxforum.org
Retail	Retail Operation http://www.nfr-arts.org
XBRL	Business Reporting and Accounting http://www.xbrl.org
NewsML	News and Publication http://www.newsml.org

Figure 26 Industry-wise Canonical Models

****

Chapter 8: MDM Implementation

8.1 Agile Development

Unlike any other technology solution, MDM is difficult for the user community to visualize, solidify and articulate. In the MDM world, Agile is about doing things quickly (and failing fast). An iterative approach enables the development team to deliver quick bursts of functional capability and receive immediate feedback from the user community to ensure that the MDM effort is focused on supporting the creation of business functionality that stakeholders need now, not at some undefined point in the future. It takes a business-first approach by understanding the business objectives and prioritizing deliverables in increments that are both measurable and validate the business value. Agile MDM recognizes that the delivery of cleansed and consistent Master Data has an evolutionary impact on the user community which will impact change in data requirements as MDM maturity grows.

The common mistake which customers are making is considering the MDM program as traditional agile. The MDM programs must be executed as Architecture-Driven Agile where system blueprints, technical architecture, and reference architectures are created before kick-off and aligned with enterprise standards and systems.

Solution architects are part of delivery teams facilitating detailed integration work and other technical "heavy lifting" for the developers. Software developers are fully attuned to the needs of the customer. The customer participates as an integral member of the development project. The IT and business units work together as part of a cross-functional, collaborative team that maintains business-focused ownership of projects and ensures that the end product meets user requirements and expectations.

Agile MDM is usage driven and not data driven. Agile implementation strategies offer significant value for MDM efforts based on incremental development, collaborative approaches to working, and focusing on providing value to the business. This approach additionally provides iterative value early and throughout the duration of the project helping to establish growing commitment from the user community as well as executive stakeholders.

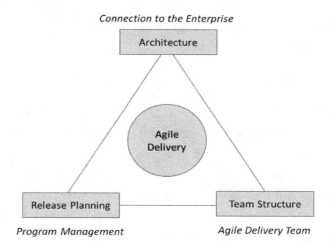

Figure 27 Architecture-Driven Agile

The benefits of Agile MDM development include

- A project is developed in rapid cycles resulting in small incremental releases with each release building on previous functionality and delivering a potentially shippable product increment.
- Agile development provides opportunities to assess the direction throughout the development lifecycle.
- Agile approach helps you achieve your enterprise master data management goals sustainably. Enhanced customer satisfaction and increased competitive gains by demonstrating and delivering MDM features as per program increment planning
- Late changes in requirements are welcomed and controlled by product backlog prioritization
- Start with a data model aligned to the business eliminating the full enterprise data model to be ready. This is a critical factor as in

some scenarios refactoring data model to accommodate change requirements leads to a major change
- Business Users will have a live MDM system to use and constant feedback from them can be incorporated into Sprint tasks.
- Better linkage between business objectives and technology requirements to ensure the right solution for the right people.
- Regular adaptation to changing circumstances
- Test-driven approach

8.2 DevOps Culture

In general, we see the IT team follows the software development model where the code is maintained in a source code repository, the build and integration team integrate the code, compiles it, and releases the package to the operations team with the deployment instructions for the next environment deployment. This process is iterative until the package is deployed into production. DevOps is a term coined by combining 'development' and 'operations'. DevOps (development and operations) is a culture, a new way of thinking. It is a set of automated software practices that combine software development (Dev), testing, and IT operations (Ops) to shorten the development cycle while delivering features, fixes, and updates frequently in alignment with the business objectives. CI/CD and DevOps are interrelated and have a common goal of making software development swift and efficient.

There exist a few differences between these two concepts. CI/CD refers to a set of development practices that enable the rapid and reliable delivery of code changes. DevOps emphasis on communication, collaboration, integration, and automation to streamline product development.

Continuous Integration (CI) is a development practice that requires developers to integrate code into a shared repository several times a day. Cl helps development teams avoid integration issues. It is about automating build and testing processes to make sure the released package is in a good state. The work of individuals is pushed into an automated system that uses scripts to build and test the code changes. After the build stage, a build server compiles the source code changes into the master code. Continuous testing offers faster bug fixes, ensures functionality, and, ultimately, results in better collaboration and software quality.

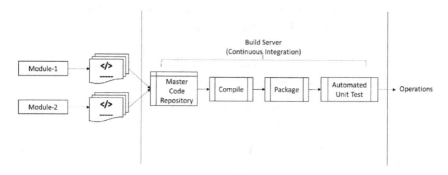

Figure 28 Continuous Integration

Continuous Delivery (CD) is the next logical step after CI. Continuous Delivery is a software development practice where software can be released into production at any time. The goal of the CD is to make sure the software is always ready to go to production with minimal effort. There is manual testing or approval before deployment to production.

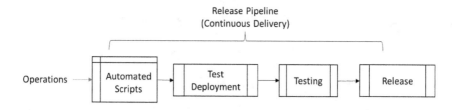

Figure 29 Continuous Delivery

Continuous Deployment (Matured Stage also called CD) - is a software development practice where software is automatically released to production continuously. With this practice, every change that passes all stages of your production pipeline is released to production. The point is to be at a state from which we can always deploy to production. There's no human intervention, and only a failed test will prevent a new change to be deployed to production. In the continuous deployment model, the users get the most up-to-date code that can pass all required tests. The organization's decision on whether to use continuous delivery or deployment depends on its business needs. Because changes are deployed to the production automatically, a continuous deployment pipeline is typically used only by DevOps teams that have a proven process.

There are plenty of ways to implement DevOps CI/CD workflows, however, continuous testing and automation are two of the most fundamental aspects of CI/CD common to all pipelines.

****

Chapter 9: Reference Data Management

Reference data is distinct from master data and metadata. Master Data provides truth, Reference Data proves context. Metadata provides meaning. Reference data is a classification scheme referred to by transactional and master records, systems, applications, processes, and reports. It is typically defined with a code and a description and has a set of domain values. As an example, the order status in the business process has values (Created | Approved | Rejected |, etc.). Some of the reference data can be universal and/or standardized (countries, industry classification, gender). Other reference data may be "agreed on" within the enterprise (customer segments, legal entity types, status codes), or within a given business domain (product classifications). Reference data is predefined read-only data that is used by consumer processes or applications transactions but not changed or modified by those transactions. It changes slowly relative to master data and often relatively static data. For example, the list of countries does not often change. Gender types do not change. For many enterprises, reference data is a major contributor to enterprise data quality problems and has a high support cost.

The demands of complying with national and international industry regulations are v the enterprises to manage and control their reference data. The CDO organizations are exploring the options to implement leading vendor COTS products as an enterprise-level initiative to reconcile cross-enterprise reference data for broader master data management initiatives and data governance structures. Reference data management solution enables a unified approach to use reference data across multiple applications, resulting in consistency and more appropriate usage of the reference data. Applications are isolated in towers and each tower solution has its representation of reference datasets with no agreed standard. It has been observed that application owners often choose reference data values that suit their needs. Enterprises in the journey of data management have put reference data management programs on priority to standardize the enterprise reference data and to centralize the management and governance of such datasets. The process controls domain values across enterprises including standardized terms, code values, business definitions, and relationships.

Organizations often create internal reference data to characterize or standardize their information which must be in sync with the RDM solution as a master-slave model. Reference data sets are also defined by external groups, such as government or regulatory bodies, to be used by multiple organizations. For example, currency codes are defined and maintained by ISO.

9.1 Solution Capabilities

Reference data platform provides a single point of management & governance for enterprise reference data. The RDM architecture is to be designed to support the use of multiple reference data domains, maintain cross-domain relationships, and adapt to changes in business needs which allow business users to define new reference data sets and manage reference data standards without requiring significant IT intervention. Defining and maintaining a canonical view of reference data sets, distributing them to downstream systems, and managing the mapping between reference data in different systems are the key patterns that need to be addressed.

- Data Definition
    - o Define
    - o Model
    - o Standardize
    - o Map
    - o Initialize
- Data Management
    - o Author
    - o Acquire
    - o Create

- o Modify
- o Delete
- o Search
- o Analyze
- o Version
- o Audit
- o Retire
- o Archive
- Data Synchronization
  - o Stage
  - o Validate
  - o Cleanse
  - o Enrich
  - o Publish

The key challenge in implementing RDM solutions is when we analyze the fact that all application towers in silos are using industry standards and using different representations for the same values. For example, the ISO 3166-1 standard defines three sets of country codes, two-letter country codes, three-letter country codes, or numeric three-digit country codes. (United States is expressed as US or USA or 840; India is expressed as IN or IND or 356). In all these scenarios, mappings must be defined to relate associated data sets. Every reference data set and mapping must be controlled by versions of reference data sets and mappings in use. Another common example is the NACE and NAICS industry codes where a reference data set contains a mapping of both industry codes. Europe supports NACE standards for industry classification. The United States supports the NAICS industry classification code. Another common disconnect is to consider reference data as it always changes slowly and is relatively static data. For example, currency exchange rates can change daily or more frequently. This type of data (Tax Rate, Exchange Rate, etc.) falls outside of the definition of reference data and does not have a predefined list of allowed values. However, like reference data, they are used by transactional applications as read-only and must be treated as reference data only.

9.2 Architecture Views

Pattern 1: Existing applications manage their Reference data to support current business. The reference data is to be synced with the RDM solution

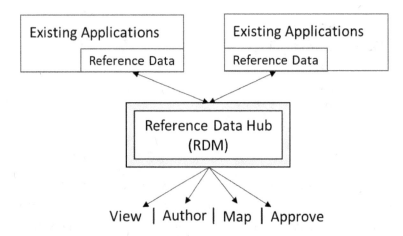

Pattern 2: Existing application sharing reference data to support other applications as is business. The reference data is to be synced with the RDM solution

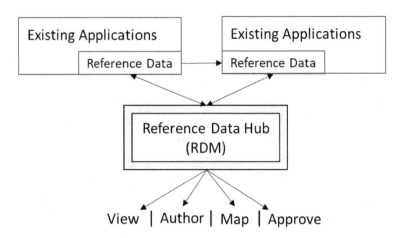

Pattern3: RDM solution provides a unified view of reference data for new applications & MDM solution

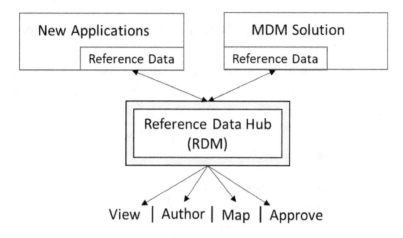

Pattern 4: RDM provides a unified view of reference data to new reports. DWH also supports existing reference data to support existing reports.

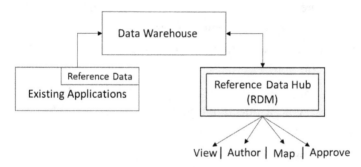

9.3 Use Cases

The common use case of an RDM solution covers

a. Centralized reference data management solution across all business functions
b. Maintaining a canonical view of reference data to create a standard across the enterprise
c. Reference data mappings across business functions to enable

reference data synchronization

d. Supports model-driven ease of deployment, implementation, and use

e. Role-based access to the reference data to all users, applications, and business processes

f. Easy import and export of reference data to and from the hub

g. Versioning and lifecycle management for reference data sets and hierarchies

h. Centralized audit, security, and stewardship processes and distribution

The below data setup for the Master data initiative is considered a Reference data setup

- Buckets
    o based on income (0-5 million; 5-10 million; and so on)
    o corporate customer size (SME, large corporate, etc.)
- Classification schemes
    o market segmentation (Personality, Gender, Demographics, Behavioral, etc.)
    o customer segmentation (High-net-worth, Mass Market, Niche Market, etc.)
    o industry classification (Manufacturing, Finance and Insurance, Educational Services, Utilities, etc.)
- Constant values
    o tax rates
    o interest rates
    o etc.
- Status codes
    o marital status
    o customer life cycle status
    o agreement status
    o etc.
- Standardized Values
    o countries

- currencies
- etc.
- Type codes
  - transaction type
  - agreement type
  - gender type
  - customer type
  - product type
  - etc.

9.4 Business Glossary

Business Metadata (Glossary) and Reference Data Management play a key role in the management of data and information for an enterprise. Reference data solution provides consistent reference data sets across multiple applications. Business Glossary provides unified standardizing definitions for that reference data. Integrating the two solutions provides the ability to manage reference data and maintain information about that reference data. It is recommended to establish a link between a reference data set and its corresponding business definition to provide clarity of terms which leads to business confidence in the quality of data sets and increases collaboration between the business and technical users. Nowadays, all industries provide a common vocabulary (business semantics) for example, the ACORD Common Business Information Glossary is a common vocabulary for the insurance industry.

****

Chapter 10: Metadata Management

The most primitive definition of Metadata is "Data about Data", i.e., description of stored data. It is information about data's meaning (semantics) and structure (syntax, constraints & relationships). This definition is not entirely inaccurate but is still insufficient from Metadata Management's point of view when the purpose is to use Metadata to drive the organization's business and operations. Forrester defines Metadata as "information that describes or provides context for data, content, business processes, services, business rules, and policies that support an organization's information systems".

Metadata describes the "What, how, when, where, and by whom, related to a particular set of data fields". Metadata provides a business glossary, how data was collected, its lineage, how data was derived, etc. Metadata plays a vital role in explaining how, why, and where data can be found, retrieved, stored, and used efficiently in an information management system. Modern data architectures enable access to a variety of data for consumers within an organization. Without a strong foundation of metadata, these architectures often show initial promise but ultimately fail to deliver. Today, even the change of a single column in a source table can impact hundreds of reports that use that data—making it extremely important to know beforehand which columns will be affected. The key focus for the metadata program includes enabling the metadata repository, governing the metadata repository, and creating an enterprise-wide data catalog to explore and search for datasets

Metadata creation and maintenance should be an integral part of the data integration processes. Metadata generation can be an exhausting process if it is performed by manually inspecting each data source. It is also required to automate the capture of metadata on the arrival of data in the MDM system and identify relationships with existing metadata definitions. Building Machine learning algorithms to auto-discover metadata and relationships is also a key aspect to consider.

This includes developing Machine Learning algorithms for "Business to Information entity to Data Entity mapping" or recommending data rules-based source data. The meta-data-driven framework is designed to enable the metadata repository, govern the metadata repository, and create an enterprise-wide data catalog to explore and search for datasets

Types of Metadata

There are three distinct types of metadata to collect: technical, operational, and business data

Technical Metadata - Captures the form and structure of each data set. It provides technical information about the data, such as the name of the source table, the source table column name, and the data type (e.g., string, integer). This is either automatically associated with a file upon ingestion or discovered manually after ingestion

Operational metadata - Describes the operational aspects of the system it represents like the date last updated, number of times accessed, frequency, latency, run time, etc.

Business metadata - Captures the business context around data, such as the business names, the descriptions of the data, the tags, owners or stewards, and associated reference data

10.1 The Solution

It is common to see different LOBs have different and sometimes conflicting definitions of apparently simple data elements. Metadata management becomes more important as repositories are integrated and shared among multiple LOBs within the organization. **Metadata management** can be defined as the end-to-end process and governance framework for creating, controlling, enhancing, attributing, defining, and managing a metadata schema, model, or another structured aggregation system, either independently or within a repository and the associated supporting processes. Enterprise-level

Metadata Management is key to building a successful Information management platform that captures, shares, displays, and secures an organization's metadata. Application developers, business users, logical modelers, and database administrators should be able to query, report, and complete impact analysis on its contents.

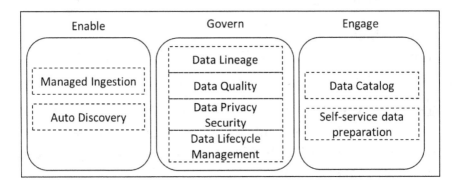

Figure 30 Solution Capabilities

The Metadata Management solution has the following capabilities-

Enable

Metadata ingestion and translation -

- Using techniques or bridges for various data sources, such as:
- Extraction, transformation, and loading (ETL); application integration; data integration; search
- Business intelligence (BI) and reporting tools
- Modeling tools
- Database management system (DBMS) catalogs
- ERP and other applications
- XML formats
- Hardware and network log files
- Microsoft Excel spreadsheets/Word documents
- PDF documents
- Business metadata
- Custom metadata

Govern

Metadata repositories - Used to document and manage metadata, and to perform analysis using the metadata. Organizations can also use repositories to publish information about reusable assets, enabling users to browse metadata during life cycle activities such as design, testing, and release management.

Business glossary - A repository used to communicate and govern the enterprise's business terms along with the associated definitions and the relationships between those terms

Data lineage - Specifies the data's origins and where it moves over time. It also describes what happens to data as it goes through diverse processes. Data lineage can help to analyze how information is used and to track key bits of information that serve a particular purpose. It is a particularly critical component of data migration since understanding the source of the data and applied transformations can be critical when interpreting information in the new repository.

Semantic frameworks - Include support for taxonomies; entity-relationship (ER) models; and ontology and modeling languages such as the Resource Description Framework (RDF), the Web Ontology Language (OWL), and the Unified Modeling Language (UML).

Engage

Impact analysis - Conveys extensive details regarding the dependencies of information or the impact of a change within a data source.

Rules management - Automates the enforcement of business rules that are tied to the data elements and associated metadata. This capability supports dedicated interfaces for the creation of, and the order of execution and links with, information stewardship for effective governance.

10.2 Maturity Model

Metadata plays a significant role in data management programs. In an organization with multiple complex systems and where people come and go frequently, metadata is essential. It adds clarity and meaning to data and helps businesspeople find what they are looking for in the way of information assets. The Metadata management maturity model gives a perspective to the organization regarding its knowledge base to handle and utilize metadata from people, processes, technology, and data point of view

There are five distinct levels of Metadata Management Maturity that an organization can attain as described below

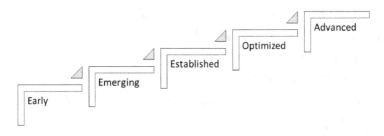

Figure 31 Levels of Metadata Management Maturity

Level 1: Early - At this level, the metadata knowledge mainly resides with the people and is created and stored locally. Sharing is ad-hoc through conversation and emails. Hence although the metadata exists in the organization it is not standardized and is of little relevant use at an organizational level.

Level 2: Emerging - At this level, the organization understands the importance of metadata and is in the discovery stage. Business consciously adds information to a central repository and starts sharing metadata for relevant use. There is no central metadata tool. Organizations may use simple tools that they already have in the organization – spreadsheets, documents, wiki pages, databases, etc. – to identify, collect, organize, and maintain metadata.

Level 3: Established - At this level, the management takes steps to educate the people across the enterprise about the importance of metadata and establish governance processes for its management. However, business units or IT silos make decisions about their metadata management systems and responsibilities without considering the broader organizational needs. Though most of these processes are non-real-time, proper metadata management tools are implemented in this stage which starts interfacing with current data through data integration and ETL tools.

Level 4: Optimized - At this level, there is a recognition of the importance of metadata management at the Chief Data Officer or equivalent level. People get imbibed with Metadata culture and constantly look to optimize the processes governing metadata management. Metadata becomes an integral part of the organization's processes, and the enterprise-wide implementation of Metadata management tools is carried out.

Level 5: Automated - At this level metadata management happens automatically as part of the business processes. All organizational metadata is stored in one common repository. Publishing and consuming metadata by all processes and systems is mandatory. People consider metadata as a critical part of organizational processes. Metadata standards are very strict, and quality is scrupulously managed. Metadata enrichment is often a well-established and automated process. Metadata can now be used across domains as it is standardized.

10.3 Metadata Management for MDM

One of the key technical drivers for MDM is the reconciliation of meanings that have diverged with distributed application development. For example, how is the term "customer" used across the organization? The definition of 'customer' for one line of business supporting retail customers in a financial organization may differ from another line of business working with government bodies for regulatory reporting. There will be scenarios where different applications use the same entity types or applications use different logical names for similar objects. Sizes and types of data are just the tip of the iceberg. The way application architectures have evolved within different divisions, there are likely going to be many ways core master objects are modeled, represented, and stored. Standardizing the business terms commonly used across the organization leveraging metadata management framework is the foundation of MDM solution. A clarified and unique view of the information about the data is a must. However, capturing metadata about every single data element identified for a master data management solution may be overwhelming and it may be advisable to initially focus on the critical data elements.

Critical Data Elements (CDEs) are defined as "the data that is critical to an organization's success" within the context of each business application use. Critical data elements help companies to quickly deliver business value by focusing on the most critical data. CDEs are used for establishing information and business policy compliance, and they must be subjected to governance in an MDM environment. The set of critical data elements can be customized to match your business requirements. As an example,

a. For analytical MDM, the CDEs to be considered are the elements used for quality analytics and reporting.
b. For operational MDM, the specific operational data elements are to be considered.
c. If the key master data management driver is compliance with regulation with "The EU General Data Protection Regulation (GDPR)", the personal data elements are to be considered as CDE
d. With BCBS 239, CDEs will be related to risk metrics or KPIs to manage business risks.
e. To identify potential duplicate records, match and merge and decisions around data survivorship, CDEs for individual

customers would be name, date of birth, address, national identifier, and gender, for an organization, name, address, or tax identification number can be considered.

10.4 Use Cases

One of the main goals of the Metadata project is to have a solution that treats information as a strategic enterprise asset, with insightful and actionable data. The new solution requires meeting the following capabilities and characteristics

a. Common, centralized business vocabulary
b. Ability to discover new or hidden business rules within the data
c. Integrate everything - Integrate with technologies like SQL, PL/SQL, various ETL tools, SAS, and others as well as build custom metadata integration solutions and provide the integrated view to discover, understand, and document source data and to map discovered data to target structures
d. Browse, explore, and search - With all the metadata gathered in a single repository now you can easily explore all the information about your databases, data files, BI reports, ETL jobs, or SQL scripts and procedures. All from a single place, accessible across your company with an intuitive web user interface.
e. Analyze end-to-end data lineage - Perform data lineage analysis to fully understand the way a particular piece of information goes through the system: down to the level of every single database column/data file field; every single component in an ETL job; every single expression is applied to the value, regardless of the technology it is being executed in
f. Perform impact analysis to control changes and prevent errors.

****

Chapter 11: Data Quality and Governance

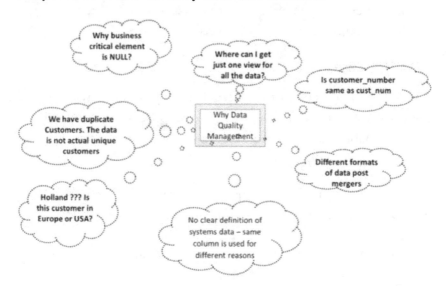

Enterprises today are struggling with the quality of data they have. It is important to understand why they get into such a mess. There are many potential reasons including excessive amounts of data collected, manual steps, unclear definitions, wrong interpretation of the fields to be filled out, and fragmentation of the information system. There would always be duplicates, missing data, corrupted text, or typo errors. Certain companies grow exponentially, and mergers and acquisitions add more quality lacking data to the pile. And above all the reasons, a common motto of "we'll cleanse the data later" is rarely achieved. The cost of not having quality data impacts company strategy and performance, business operations, IT operations, and compliance. Low data quality can take many shapes; not just incorrect figures, but a lack of completeness, or the data being too old (for meaningful use), loss of customer satisfaction, high running costs, inefficient decision-making processes, and performance.

Master Data Management solutions have elevated the importance of information quality. Data quality is one of the key components of a master data governance initiative.

11.1 Data Quality

The quality and correctness of data is the major contributing factor to achieving the "golden record" or "single view". Data quality processes for MDM ensure data integrity, completeness, standardization, validation, stewardship, record timeliness, and accuracy. It can be managed using a toolbox of sub-disciplines that includes Data Catalog, Data Profiling, Data Cleansing, and Data Matching. There is a general perception that by realizing MDM tools, the organization immediately benefits in Data Quality and Governance which is not always true. Data quality is both a technical and a business issue and if not managed properly, it would be garbage in – garbage out scenario.

The studies of data quality mainly focused on the data value (which covers data status quality and data service quality) and data structure governed by the data management process. As an example,

a. the fields customer_id and cust_id may or may not all refer to the same type of data.
b. "customer_id" and "customer_ID" are spelled the same but are not the same. "customer_id" is a legacy key and "customer_ID" is mapped to a government identification number. (ex. SSN)
c. Just because a field is named FK_CUSTOMER doesn't mean that it is a foreign key to the customer table.

11.1.1 Data Quality Dimensions

We can measure data quality on multiple dimensions with equal or varying weights. Data quality dimensions serve as a guide for selecting the most suitable dataset. When presented with two datasets of 79% accuracy and 92% accuracy, analysts can choose the dataset with higher accuracy to ensure that their analysis has a more trusted foundation. The following key dimensions are used.

Accuracy is the degree of closeness of data values to real values. Accuracy is connected to precision, reliability, and veracity. Address cleansing, name and address standardization, demographic matching, and valid phone numbers are all examples of accuracy checks

Availability is the degree to which data can be consulted or retrieved by data consumers or a process. For example, verifying emails, phone numbers, and access to reference tables.

Clarity is the ease with which data consumers can understand the metadata. The aim here is to understand the meaning of the data. For example, for two addresses given, clarity is a must to define one as the billing address and the other as the delivery address.

Consistency is the degree to which the same information stored and used at multiple instances matches. The aim is to identify where different values of the same record are present. For example, the same customer gender is stored as "Male" in one system and "NA" in the other. Is the same invoice number referenced with two different amounts?

Currency is the degree to which data values are up to date.

Punctuality is the degree to which the period between the actual and target point of time of availability of a dataset is appropriate

Timeliness is the degree to which the period between the time of the creation of the real value and the time that the dataset is available is appropriate. For example, as per company policy, prospects older than one year are to be shelved and cannot be considered in identifying the life cycle of a customer.

Traceability is the degree to which data lineage is available. The purpose is to understand the origin of data and the transformation rules between source data and target data. Many data quality problems can be traced to incorrect loads, missed loads, or system failures that go unnoticed

Completeness is the degree to which all required data are present.

The purpose is to identify the empty, null, or missing data. For example, missing critical data elements. e.g., a complete address would contain the street address, city, state, and zip code

Uniqueness is the degree to which records occur only once in a data file. The aim is to ensure the data is not duplicated. For example, identify cases where the same communication is going to the customer multiple times as there are multiple records available. The completeness and uniqueness of data quality dimensions must be solved with either extended data models and/or alternative methodologies.

Integrity, Does the actual data match our description of the data? integrity checks examine whether the data is complete. These checks ensure that source and target count matches cardinality checks, linkages, and referential integrity. e.g., if you have contact information not associated with a party, the data is invalid

Validity is the degree to which data values comply with rules. For example, an invalid email format. Misspelled reference data ("Prospect" is misspelled as "Pospect" in a few instances). Data structures play a significant role and there are intersections with data quality. The data integrity and validity dimension are closely related to data structure and a given data model can impact these data quality dimensions.

The dimensions of data quality are classified by data concept. The following data concepts are distinguished

a. Data covers quality dimension **Availability**
b. Data file covers quality dimension **Traceability**
c. Data value covers quality dimension **Accuracy, Completeness, Consistency, Currency, Validity, Integrity**
d. Dataset availability covers quality dimensions **Punctuality, Timeliness**
e. Metadata covers quality dimension **Clarity**

f.   Record covers quality dimension **Completeness, Uniqueness**

11.1.2 Data Quality – Five-Step Process

(1) Data Profiling

Data Profiling is the use of analytical techniques on data to capture insight into the quality of data and help to identify data quality issues. The aim is to develop a thorough knowledge of its content, structure, and quality. The data profiling program includes structural analysis of the data stores, pattern analysis, range, or threshold analysis for required fields, analysis of counts like record count, sum, mode, minimum, maximum, percentiles, mean and standard deviation, and cross-table (or cross-system) relationship identification.

(2) Data Parsing

Parsing of data allows us to compare individual components and create meaningful metadata-driven data. Inconsistent structure and formats, and misfielded words are typically challenging situations to deal with where business rules are introduced to get value out of data.

Input Data	Parsed Data
John Smith, Sales Head Customer Services Lake View Building 11400 Lake House Holland US 24568 205369852	Name : John Smith Title : Sales Head Department : Customer Services Location: Lake View Building Number: 11400 County: Lake House City: Holland Country: US ZIP: 24568 Phone: 205369852

(3) Data Correction

The process to cleanse and validate the data. In the below example le, address, country, and zip code are cleansed and validated. This may be using in-house systems or third-party services for address correction.

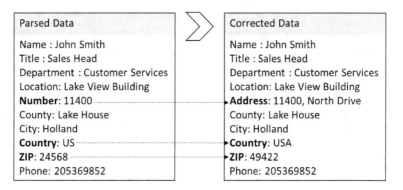

(4) Data Standardization

The process to arrange information into a preferred and consistent format. In the below example, the name is standardized as title, first name, and last name. The phone is standardized with country code.

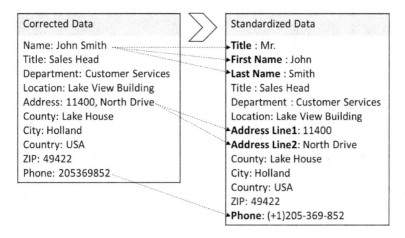

(5) Data Matching / Merging

Data Matching and Merging are two different tasks. Data Matching (Suspect Identification) is the process to identify multiple records that may represent the same entity based on rules on critical data elements. Data Merging is a comparison of identified suspects' data based on business rules and creates a merged profile.

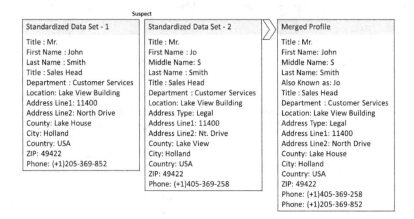

11.1.3 Data Quality Monitoring

The data patterns and the format of data play a significant role in compliance with the quality of data. Identifying the root cause requires knowledge of which application is the source of truth and the lineage of data. The most critical component of data quality metrics is the ability to collect the statistics associated with data quality metrics and establish governance that enables action to be taken. Businesses having a lack of confidence in their data quality can jeopardize the future of AI in their organization. The reliability of the data can directly impact the success of AI models. Deploying statistical techniques ensures continuous monitoring of data quality and establishes control limits.

Data Monitoring solution provides the ability to measure the health and usage of data by automated logging and tracing of the data and data pipelines to evaluate data quality and identify issues. The Data quality scorecard can be presented by scoring for a data set's conformance within each dimension of data quality and by integrating the data profiling and cleansing outcomes within the dashboard application to track data quality improvement over time by comparing historical views. For a data-driven organization, it is the responsibility of the IT team, data team, analytics team, and domain team to ensure needed collaboration and focus on managing and using structured data. The IT team can deploy the solution to monitor data quality, but they need recommendations from other teams about what to monitor, build the data pipelines, build analytics and AI/ML models to analyze and interpret data and make business decisions.

Data Quality Dimensions						
KPI	Completeness	Integrity	Consistency	Timeliness	Uniqueness	Accuracy
Overall Customer Data	90%	88%	72%	89%	92%	68%
Customer						
Name	92%	92%	92%	92%	92%	92%
Email	86%	86%	86%	86%	86%	86%
Date of Birth	94%	94%	94%	94%	94%	94%
Gender Code	88%	88%	88%	88%	88%	88%
Vendor						
Vendor Code	80%	80%	80%	80%	80%	80%
Vendor Name	100%	100%			100%	100%
Brand Name	90%	90%	90%	90%	90%	90%
Payment Method	90%	90%	90%	90%	90%	90%
Product Code	90%	90%	90%	90%	90%	90%

Figure 32 Sample Data Quality Dashboard

11.2 Data Governance

Data Governance creates a culture, where creating and maintaining high-quality data is a core discipline of the organization. It is the orchestration of people, processes, and technology to enable an organization to leverage information as an enterprise asset.

a. From a people standpoint, it necessitates the combined effort from both business and IT when addressing the myriad of quality issues throughout the enterprise.

b. From a process perspective, it also demands IT and business to engage in a truly collaborative effort, without so much of the commonly seen politics and obstacles generally imposed in their relationships.

c. Finally, technology, when applied properly, can expedite problem resolution as well as make it viable to establish a mature and repeatable process.

The most common definitional mistake companies make is using "data governance" synonymously with "data management." Data governance is the "decision rights and policy making" for corporate data, while data management is the "tactical execution" of those policies.

With respect to Master data, the Data Governance process also called Master Data Governance (MDG) ensures that the master data in an organization meets the expectations of all the business purposes, in the context of data quality, data stewardship, ownership, compliance, privacy, security, data risks, and data sensitivity. This also includes "gating" mechanisms for approvals, defined roles and responsibilities, training plans to ensure the correct level of skills are provided, and a communication plan to ensure stakeholders are kept informed and decisions can be made in a timely manner.

The data governance programs eventually address the following activities

a. Defining/aligning policies, standards, and rules
b. Establish key metrics, monitors, and improvement targets
c. Identify data entry points
d. Establish quality and service level agreements
e. Define metadata management plan
f. Communicating with data stakeholders

To some extent, it is data governance requirements that are converted to business requirements for MDM. This includes -

a. Identify enterprise data to be moved into the master data management system
b. Initial and ongoing sources of master data
c. Quality of master data of each repository
d. Ongoing measurement and management of quality of data
e. The process to review and approve master data changes and the potential roles in MDM
f. Enabling monitoring and reconciliation of data between MDM and its sources and consumers
g. Data refinement, standardization, and aggregation activities along the path of the end-to-end information flow
h. Common definitions for the semantics, structure, and services for the master data domains
i. Maintaining Metadata, reporting on data lineage, or ongoing data quality management with regular profiling
j. Elimination of duplicate entries and creation of linking and matching keys
k. Define the mechanisms that create and maintain cross-reference linkages between MDM and other systems
l. Supports manual corrections of false positive and negative matches that cannot be managed automatically.
m. Archiving of master data and relevant transactional data by defined archiving policies

The Master Data Governance control process is generally implemented in three models

a. Cross-functional
b. Subject Area
c. Centralized or as a combination.

The Cross-Functional teams are formed to coordinate standards and integrations for the cross-project integrations around data. The Subject Area teams are formed around individual subject areas across enterprises to establish business ownership of data decisions independent of projects. The Central group centralizes all major data decisions and maintains all data assets. The team is formally known as 'data stewards' and the process are called 'data stewardship'.

Good data governance is to understand what data is vital to the health and welfare of the business, drive improvements to the quality and availability of the data to make these assets more valuable, and ensure there is ongoing budgeting and caretaking to maintain the health and integrity of these assets. Governing the creation, management, and usage of enterprise data is not an option any longer. It is expected by customers, demanded by executives, and enforced by regulators/auditors. Not only master data governance but there is also governance required in related disciplines as well within the MDM project life cycle which includes IT governance and SOA governance. IT Governance covers the aspects of the availability and security of information as well as some aspects of the data life cycle. There are several standards related to IT Governance; the most often referenced for regulatory compliance is the COBIT (Control Objectives for Information and Technology) from the IT governance institute. SOA governance covers the nature of the services to be exposed to consuming applications, deciding if the service is available only to internal consumers or to consumers outside the organization, specifying security to define who can see what, and the parameters to retire or revamp existing services.

11.2.1 Data Stewardship and Data Ownership

The concept of data stewardship is different from data ownership. Data stewards do not own the data. Their role is to ensure that adequate, agreed-upon quality metrics are maintained continuously. Data stewards work closely with the information technology group to discover and mitigate the risks introduced by inadequate data quality. While reviewing the models, it is important to evaluate which model works well and leverages current organizational structures and systems. The cross-functional model is based on data requirements for each initiative with distributed responsibilities and may not recognize enterprise-level requirements. The subject area driven model promotes consistency across initiatives as the data definitions, standards, and decisions are business driven. Within the centralized model, the governance team maintains the enterprise data model and other data assets and encourages collaboration across projects.

11.3 Tools and Technologies

The data governance issues must be owned by both IT and business. The business side of the equation must define the governing rules and processes; the IT side must provide the tools and systems to automate the processes. The organization leverages data management technologies to support the governance processes ranging from data discovery, data profilers, master data management, metadata repositories, monitoring tools, tools to manage the information life cycle, and governance dashboards.

The tools and technologies include-

Data Catalog, the platform is the source of records for all metadata (i.e.: business glossary, business rules, governance policies, etc.) within an enterprise. The data catalog tool provides a unified metadata view to the user which helps them to find, understand and trust the data source. The recent COTS products available in the market are AI-powered tools, supporting patterns to identify technical metadata, relationships, and usage. Organizations today are considering data catalog initiatives as separate initiatives for identifying metadata resources and cataloging, practicing information governance, orchestrating people, processes, data, and technology, and developing a metadata-driven vision.

Data Discovery is used to identify data insights from hidden patterns and trends and propagate the results into a data quality metrics repository

Data profiling is used to analyze metadata, assess the quality of data and, importantly, identify data quality business rules

Master Data Management is used to have a single view of data, manage relationships, and hierarchies, and identify and eliminate duplicate data.

Critical data elements and their definitions are managed within a metadata repository. ·

Incident management applications are retooled to support the reporting and tracking of data quality issues and their resolutions.

Information life cycle (ILM) is a systematic, policy-based approach to the information collection, use, retention, and deletion

Governance portals provide a front end to data stewards for drilling down, evaluating, and perhaps even correcting data flaws. Data quality metrics are accumulated and reported within a business intelligence platform for presenting dashboards and scorecards.

****

Chapter 12: MDM for Analytics

Business data analytics is a specific set of techniques, competencies, and practices, applied to perform continuous exploration, investigation, and visualization of business data. It is a management discipline that looks at how to organize the process, how to ask the right questions, how to select the techniques and approaches, and how to interpret the results of data analysis specific to the business context to drive meaningful decisions and to make conclusions. The analytics solution deals with transactional and master data to consolidate critical information which is foundational to key business processes for an organization. The master data objects produce "dimensions", and the facts are produced using transactional data, providing the basic framework for performing analytics to improve productivity, efficiency, and positive financial outcomes.

MDM vendors have realized the potential of analytics on master data and have facilitated the analytical solutions integrated with MDM platforms to provide insight into the MDM processes, and potential issues & improvements over time. For example, the integrated analytical solution monitors how well the master data is being managed, how many new customers have been created, daily changes to master data unique customers we have, and the non-functional use cases like time for batch process.

MDM integration with data warehouses, data lakes, online transaction processing (OLTP), online analytical processing (OLAP) applications, data streams, and other variety of sources provides the complete analytical solution and builds predictive models leveraging the governance and quality benefits associated with MDM. With proper governance and oversight, the data in the master data system (or repository, or registry) can be qualified as a unified and coherent data asset that all applications can rely on for consistent, high-quality information.

There are many analysis possibilities we can apply to data supported by multiple user-friendly tools for data analysis and visualization. On one side it lowers the bar for quantitative investigations and data-driven decisions, but on the other hand, it comes with risks because people can run analyses without understanding business and data, resulting in the risk of making poor decisions.

The concept of data science works with Business Analytics. Data Science involves a combination of technical skills such as modeling, statistics, analytics, and mathematics that are used together to solve business problems. Business data analytics is a process discipline that takes input from data science and works with that input to help make decisions. Most business decisions involve some degree of uncertainty and data plays a crucial and transformational role in helping decision-makers navigate through that uncertainty.

There are four types of analytics methods in general: descriptive, diagnostic, predictive, and prescriptive.

a. Descriptive analytics - What has happened - Provides insight into the past by describing or summarizing data. It aims to answer the question
b. Diagnostic analytics - The why behind the what - It is important to understand the cause of the root cause of it.
c. Predictive analytics - what is likely to happen - Analyze data trends to provide insights into the future. For example, predict your profits and losses based on your previous financial performance.
d. Prescriptive analytics - What should happen if we do this – it uses the findings from different forms of analytics to quantify the anticipated effects and outcomes of specific decisions or events.

The rise or fall of your business lies in data. The following quote sums up perfectly the need for data in a business, "Knowing where you're going is the first step in getting there.". On average, that's 2.5 quintillion bytes of data every single day. It's a million, million, million data points. Data useful to business comes in different forms.

The analysis of the data can be conducted in many business contexts using a variety of different methods. These methods come from both classical statistics as well as from artificial intelligence. Cluster detection, Regression, Neural networks, decision trees, and link analysis are a few algorithms used commonly. Data Science and machine learning are crucial facets of Information Management and the Big Data world, helping enterprises in making data-driven decisions and creating data products (algorithms). Google page rank algorithm, suggesting corrections to misspelled searches, Facebook, and LinkedIn patterns to suggest other people you may know, Amazon product recommendations based on search, and so on are a few of the examples of data products.

12.1 Analytics Use Cases

Analytics Adoption in Banking

Banks are implementing analytical solutions to acquire targeted customers, inhibiting churn, new product launches, personalized customer experience, credit default risk mitigation, and fraud detection where the MDM system plays a significant role by creating golden records for customers, products, locations, and agreements with quality data leveraging machine learning algorithms. As an example, the analytics on the frequency of customer interaction with banks (stored in MDM as customer interaction) gives views on unhappy customers, their changing demands, and insights into how customers' preferences are evolving. Another view is analytics on customer lifetime value, brand loyalty, and product demand based on customers in the geographical area

Analytics Adoption in Insurance

Insurers today focus on understanding customer needs and sentiments. The MDM program enables a 360-degree view of customer demographic information, customer financial profile, preferences, products, interactions, campaigns, and claim management which helps in predicting customer behavior and generating personalizing offers. Analytics on customer financial profiles would play a big role in the Insurance industry. Cross-sell insurance products to customers in the same household (MDM householding capability) facilitates driving the revenue

Analytics Adoption in Healthcare and Life Sciences

The MDM programs cover Member, Consumer, Patient, Organization, Product, and Reference data. The data and analytics journey realizes the full value of data assets using MDM across all lines of business. Analytics on patient history to improve the life of patients, analytics on treatment for the same problem to offer the best treatment, uncovering hidden patterns from clinical data, and patient behavior are a few of the benefits. Electronic health records, type of disease, provider details, and other parameters help in better clinical design patterns. The product MDM implementation plays a crucial role in analytics on Drug effectiveness and drug discovery

Analytics Adoption in Retail

The Customer, Item, and Supplier MDM programs in the Retail segment support analytics for enterprise initiatives such as digital strategy, customer experience management, loyalty, and promotions. The implementation of analytics use cases enables the "Segment of One approach" in the retail industry to cover product recommendations leveraging intelligent product searches and deep learning, chatbots, and virtual personal assistants to achieve fully integrated omnichannel presence, predictive modeling on historical sales, demand forecasting, measuring lost sales, customers buying behavior, optimize cost by doing analytics on store operational hours about customer inflow and enable new suppliers' tie-ups based on manufacturing location product cost and touchpoint in terms of Buying, Shipping, Invoicing, Payments.

12.2 MDM Analytics Initiative and Benefit

Customer Optimization

a. Improve up-sell, cross-sell, and customer retention

b. Access full-customer view
  - Transactions, products, and interactions
  - Understand customer lifetime value
  - Leverage relationships and areas of influence
  - Provide customer experience equal to customer value
  - Segment customers accurately
  - Improve customer interaction
  - Improve marketing effectiveness

Operational Efficiency

a. Send the right marketing and compliance materials to the right people in the right place
b. Improve reporting processes – easier, faster, and more accurate
c. Reduce business process exceptions from inaccurate, conflicting data
d. React more quickly to events and changes

Risk Management

a. Monitor complex fraud patterns across products, systems, divisions, and geographies
b. Gain visibility into customer credit risk across financial and accounting systems
c. Analyze product risk across distribution channels, uses, and geographies

Regulatory Compliance

a. Manage opt-in preferences across product lines and geographies
b. Ensure privacy rules are managed
c. Manage industry-specific compliance, such as Basel I, II, and III and BCBS 239 (banking) and HIPAA (insurance)

12.3 Data Storytelling

The common theme that cuts across movies, books, and documentaries is the stories. The human brain is evolved to understand stories. An unordered list of facts is hard to remember, and this is the same for data which affects our lives in more ways than we can imagine and every year we consume more and more of it. These days, the world runs on data. The data is to be presented, memorable and interpreted and the best way is to tell a story using the language of data to help businesses. Data is the new essence of business, and visualization has emerged as the common language. Speaking, this language is not about learning numbers or statistics. It's more about visual thinking and storytelling skills applied to graphs and charts. The goal of data visualization is to communicate information clearly and effectively to an audience so they can decide based on facts. It is a critical step in the data science process. With large data sets visualization helps in understanding complex data relationships and data-driven insights by use of visual objects such as the points, lines, and bars on a graph.

Data visualization refers to the techniques used to communicate data and information and usually falls under three categories

a. Information Visualization (Exploratory Analysis)
b. Scientific Visualization (Confirmatory Analysis)
c. Visual Analytics (Presentation)

Information Visualization typically involves abstract information, and non-physically based data to amplify perception. For example, a Graph of stock prices or an Analysis of product-wise sales for Retail stores. Scientific visualization involves explaining the data that have a physical position in place. For example, an earthquake simulation data set where each set has a 3D location. Visual analytics is the science of analytical reasoning supported by interactive visual interfaces. Visual analytics uses data analytics and interactive visual representations of the data and dashboarding to enable users to interpret large volumes of data. For example, searching for insights into the data.

With the Data modernization journey, the organization today claims to have control over data and become more reliant on data they have, and with the increase in the number of people who are fluent in the language of data, more and more reports are being created in the workplace. For a successful data visualization journey, it is important to investigate what is being used, consolidated or can be done better. Completing a report rationalization will help to figure out commonly used reports and identify clean-up and priority areas. Storytelling with data is the art of showing different perspectives to different audiences. Business is interested in something if it has suggestions for organizational growth and financial savings and we can only get attention if we understand the organization's business and data and by making a connection between the audience and the data during data storytelling.

The data is the real story, and you need to keep your audience engaged. With great data comes great responsibility so misleading your audience by fabricating data is unethical behavior. Be honest about what the data show, what can be concluded from the data, and what the data limitations are. If there is a need to make up data for showing some examples, the disclaimer is important to communicate. If you are honest about the data, then your audience will trust and respect you. Before starting the visualization, ask yourself what you are trying to achieve with this analysis. It is always a promising idea to onboard a business from day one to understand what the business wants to communicate. Choosing the right visualization, right colors, informative title, adding legends, and ensuring each piece of analysis and data story should ultimately have a point that resonates with an audience. We can see diverse ways of data visualizations in our daily routines' newspapers publish a lot of data in form of graphs. Data visualization in gas and electricity bills showing bar charts, and pie charts. Banking apps showing spending patterns. Smartwatches show steps you have done, the number of calories, and so on. Travel website ratings for food service and values and atmosphere are represented using our bar chart.

****